ADVANCE PRAISE FOR
TERRAFORM

"Brilliant, searing, and completely new, Prop doesn't just teach us about terraforming, he literally terraformed something new and generous—and funny!—with this book. It will give you a whole language and lens for cocreation of a more beautiful and true world."

—SARAH BESSEY, *New York Times* bestselling author of *A Rhythm of Prayer*

"The culture is at an inflection point and we need voices that can rightly interpret the times, voices that can inspire humanity to move forward. In walks Propaganda with the fire of a Black prophet and a tongue sharp like a sword ready to do the painstaking work of terraforming our souls. *Terraform* is gritty, masterful, and wholly transcendent."

—WILLIAM MATTHEWS, artist and advocate, singer-songwriter, cohost of *The Liturgists* podcast

"Propaganda brings the gifts of his brilliant thoughts and powerful words into a book that not only inspires us to believe that we can re-create a world in which beauty and justice flourish but gives us the tools to do so."

—JENNY YANG, vice president of advocacy and policy, World Relief

"What is this book? Is it poetry? Prose? Wild ramblings? Social commentary? Inspiration? Provocation? Yes to all of it. Yes to Prop's beautiful, faithful imagination and to his sharp-eyed, openhearted observation of the world around us. Yes to his gorgeous call to dream, to cherish, to remember, to breathe, to love."

—JEFF CHU, cocurator of Evolving Faith and author of *Does Jesus Really Love Me?*

"Propaganda weaves together words, as only he can, to stir up our discontent for the current state of things and help us form a vision for a better future. *Terraform* is a brilliant road map for reconstructing the world written by one of our generation's most spiritually subversive poets. We ignore it at our peril."

—JONATHAN MERRITT, contributing writer for *The Atlantic* and author of *Learning to Speak God from Scratch*

"Propaganda's brilliant prose crystallizes into this refreshing, comprehensive guide for anyone who has yearned to transform themselves and their communities."

—IAN MORGAN CRON, author of *The Story of You* and coauthor of *The Road Back to You*

TERRAFORM

TERRAFORM

BUILDING A BETTER WORLD

·PROPAGANDA·

HarperOne
An Imprint of HarperCollins*Publishers*

TERRAFORM. Copyright © 2021 by Propaganda DBA. All rights reserved. Printed in the United States of America. No part of this book may be used or reproduced in any manner whatsoever without written permission except in the case of brief quotations embodied in critical articles and reviews. For information, address HarperCollins Publishers, 195 Broadway, New York, NY 10007.

HarperCollins books may be purchased for educational, business, or sales promotional use. For information, please email the Special Markets Department at SPsales@harpercollins.com.

FIRST EDITION

Designed by SBI Book Arts, LLC

Library of Congress Cataloging-in-Publication Data has been applied for.

ISBN 978-0-06-303624-6

21 22 23 24 25 LSC 10 9 8 7 6 5 4 3 2 1

Lighters up, everyone . . .

To DJ Efechto,

Kobe,

Nipsey,

David Reynosa

and everyone who ever wanted to run to
the middle of the street and shout

IT DOESN'T HAVE TO BE THIS WAY!

Aṣẹ

CONTENTS

FOREWORD

I was sitting in the green room—that catered, behind-the-scenes scene every big concert or conference has for hosting and hiding "the talent" from the masses out front—when Jason "Propaganda" Petty sat down beside me. Or maybe I sat beside him. But who approached who doesn't matter—it was the look we shared that made the moment. The look that said, "Do all these people think this is real?"

Someone famous was on stage.

Prop was about to perform next.

And the energy of the arena, with its staff and security, All Access passes, the coterie and sycophants, screamed, "I feel so lucky to be here!"

We'd give high fives and fist bumps when someone came offstage, but given our roads to get here and the people we were returning home to, the pomp didn't hold much sway.

Prop says the question "Where you from?" is shorthand for "Did you survive anything?" And if our initial handshake didn't say enough, I think I got my pass when I told him I was fresh off the plane from my home in Iraq, where the terror group ISIS was waging a relentless takeover of the country and Syria, and knocking on Europe's door from the shores of North Africa. So while the son of a Black Panther from South Central LA and the son of a white preacher from Texas wouldn't appear to have a lot in common, we felt a mutual respect over all we'd both survived, and immediately realized no one else in that room could understand us like we could understand each other.

We'd survived some stuff.

In fact, the violence is why I was invited into these rooms at all.

"Jeremy, help us understand ISIS and what we can do to stop them and protect those suffering from their genocide." Depending on the room, it was a foreign policy question, a religious freedom question, or a human rights question. Regardless, it was always a shortsighted question.

"Well, you're a few decades too late for that," would be my typical response, as though decades of domestic and foreign policy, colonialism, corruption, theological bigotry, and ethnic conflicts could be cured before the next quarterly report was due, when we all got bored again and moved on.

As with police violence against Black men, the caging of Latino migrant children, demonization of queer folk, and exploitation of the ecosystems that sustain us, society at large typically only finds its conscience after decades of tending the garden we suddenly want to uproot. The headlines find us flat-footed, looking at our perfectly pruned bonsai trees indignantly: *Who planted this?! Don't you know I'm anti-bonsai?!*

But it's always us. We did it. After decades of policy and centuries of thought, suddenly we want to solve it overnight, ideally without disrupting the things that are working for the most comfortable among us.

Prop and I became friends over our shared realities of violence, and our shared need to dispel the stereotypes about the places we each called "home." South Central was little more than riots, drugs, and gangs to me. Iraq was little more than war, oil, and terrorists to him. But we knew our caricatures were wrong, and we forged our friendship turning over every rock of the stories we'd been handed about "those people," in search of the truth. When I said ISIS was about young men having purpose and a place to belong more than millenarian apocalyptic theology, he got it immediately.

"Oh. It's a gang. Word."

It may not be a coincidence that Prop's crowning work to date, *Crooked*, is populated with Iraq War veterans, refugees, PTSD, the military-industrial complex, and the duplicity of an American evangelicalism that prays for peace while giving a middle finger to its neighbor. And it's certainly no mistake that my work over this period became more explicit and informed in pursuing justice, equality, and dignity for Black people and LGBTQ+ people across the world. These were our conversations. We learned and grew up together, both becoming more informed and refined as we leaned into the oppression and trauma that affected our families and our friends.

But "Propaganda" is a bit of persona. And I love that guy. But it's *Jason Petty* to whom I owe so much. Off duty. After hours. When the crowds are gone. The late-night texts and calls across the ocean. The guy I can dream with and the one who makes me a better leader.

So when I commend this book to you, I'm doing so because I trust Jason and I can speak firsthand to the impact the ideas and thoughts in this book have had on my life, before they were ever written down. And I do so from my vantage point as a humanitarian peace practitioner on the front lines of violence. This book is of the streets, for the streets.

Words like *war* and *gang violence, wild fires* and *hurricanes* cause us to despair at the random nature of their chaos and senselessness. But we get it wrong. ISIS and police violence, famines and refugee crises are neither random nor senseless. They are not weeds that crop up overnight. They are carefully planted, curated realities—*bonsai*; they are choices. And these headline-making choices will not be overturned by conferences or concerts or crocodile tears. They require a rethinking of *everything*. And that is the invitation Jason makes in this book.

It's easy to miss it, but even in his stage name, Jason has been urging us to ask what's real, shrug off the hype, and challenge the indoctrination. Baiting us, mocking us, warning us as we bob our heads, literally, to Propaganda . . .

Are you seeing things for what they really are?
Do you know what you're consuming?
And how do you know what you know?

We don't just "get free."
We have to see it.
We have to choose it.
We have to risk it.
Or we lose it.

So if you're tired of The Way Things
*   Are . . .*
If you're ready to make the world livable,
*   for all of us—*
The World Where Everything Rises . . .
Read on. Jason Petty's going to show the way.

Terraform.

> —Jeremy Courtney
> CEO, Preemptive Love Coalition
> Author, *Love Anyway*
> Iraq
> December 2020

TERRAFORM

MISSION TO MARS

WORDS BUILD WORLDS

Last night I asked Normal
"How come you never have to explain yourself?"
She sighed,
Looked a little frightened
"I was just about to ask you the same question"

BIG HOMIE,
TERRAFORM . . . HUH?!

Who names a book *Terraform*?! Sheesh! My friends say I'm a unicorn. What son of a Black Panther who speaks Spanish and enjoys a good Sufjan Stevens song also knows what "What the lick read?" means? I can politic about politics, supralapsarianism, why Brooklyn can claim to be the coolest uncle of hip-hop, the cooling temperature of magma, and the Magna Carta. I can tell you how and when Gandalf went from the grey to the white, who was the second king of ancient Mali, and the difference between South American and African coffee by smell. My friend Lecrae once said, "Yo, Prop the type of dude to, on Juneteenth, eat a fried catfish taco with a craft beer." I was shook at how accurate that was. They say unicorn, I say striving to be fully earthling.

Earth! Amiright?! All of it, the entire human experience . . . here. Sitting on a rock that ain't even the center of its own solar system, which ain't in the center of its galaxy. Still, all that Earth is, its entire structure and formation, we had nothing to do with. I mean, look, vegetation is kinda magical. We just put seeds in the ground and it makes plants. Then, the plants make oxygen. Nobody told it to. Earth just does what it does.

"Wow that's interesting."
"What is?"
"All of it."

However, what it means to be an earthling, that's on us. There is so much that we are, and have been, and could be. This thing called existence is so weird. So many things about Earth and earthlingness are just absolutely preposterous. I find that I just can't shake my gaze. Y'all say unicorn, I say full earthling.

In science fiction, when someone discovers a distant planet that could possibly sustain life yet is still too hostile an environment for humans in its current state, a team of scientists and engineers must work over decades, or maybe centuries, to make the air breathable, the ground fertile, and the climate more suitable for human flourishing. They must get that rock to do what Earth does naturally. This process is called terraforming. It is what the Nat Geo show *Mars* is based on. It is exactly what may someday happen on actual Mars if humans ever start a colony on that currently uninhabitable planet.

So here's my metaphor. What if we applied the idea of terraforming to our world today? What if you could terraform the culture, your family, your

inner world, and yourself? What if the interplan-
etary scientists and engineers were actually earth-
ling artists, songwriters, and poets? Let me take the
metaphor even further—what if we thought about
our cultural climate in the same way we consider
the actual climate, and the harvestable ground was
actually represented by the ideas we plant in others'
hearts and minds? What if the air we breathe was
represented by the songs, poems, and stories we
sing over each other? What if our words created
worlds? Now, here is the gut punch: that's exactly
what we have been doing the whole time.

We make culture.
Culture makes us.
Rinse and repeat.

In *The Sacred Canopy*, the sociologist Peter
Berger asserts that humans are the only species
not born with everything they need to survive.
We actually have to create other things to survive,
such as language, both written and spoken, family
structure, and art and music. In other words, cul-
ture doesn't exist in nature; we make it.

Then something magical happens. Soon after
we make culture, culture makes us. Think about

it! Who is your mom's brother to you? Your uncle, of course. Why?! What does that guy have to do with you?! Well, in a hunter-gatherer nomadic society, familial ties are crucial to build trust and safety, which heightens the chances of survival. I can trust this dude not to feed me a poison berry because, well, I'm his nephew, he'll take care of me. So for survival, we invented the extended family. I can't stress this enough: we made it up! Then, in the way that culture works, what we made up started to make us.

IMMA

Imma alter your summer solstice
Imma builder of all cultures
Imma cosmic explorer
Build a new habitat
terraform.
Imma outlaw Seasons, specifically cuffin.
You gotta force love you got nothin,
I got Earth Science
Modern Mayan
Early Druid
building blocks
Nitrogen = humility
Oxygen = civility

Here is an example closer to us in time. I like to call myself an OS1 Millennial. I'm like the first iPhone of Millennials. I had an analog early childhood but digital young adulthood. There was a time when I memorized all the phone numbers of my friends and family. A time that I had to know the streets I was on and took my best guess as to which route would have the least traffic to get home. Now, I couldn't memorize a phone number if you had a Second Amendment right all up on my forehead! The only number I know is my wife's. My daughter, she's out of luck! If I'm touring and my phone dies, I have zero idea how to get to the airport!

I feel like my brain honestly can't do these tasks anymore. Why? Smartphones have completely rewired our brain's neural passages. Where we used to dedicate space for remembering important information, we now use our phone's memory to store it for us. We thought we were clearing hard drive space off our brains by making the phones do these tasks. All we did was fill that space up with memes and GIFs (also made up by us). And now all this has made us! Tech terraformed us. It changed our language: we now say things like LOL but don't actually laugh, or we legit lose friends because the tone of our text message was misread. Technology has reshaped our cognitive abilities and how we navigate our space. Something we made is making us now.

IF WE AIN'T CAREFUL

If we aren't careful
Mars will just be another gold rush.
Another pre-Columbian America
Scraping
Raping
Scratching
Gouging
Making up lines and screaming "mine" into
*   newly made oxygen*
Tapping Planetary vein in search of arrogance in
*   the form of rocks,*
Imaginary wealth.
You know the actual millionaires of the gold rush
*   were the shovel salesmen?*
You went about this all wrong
Mars finna another East India Trade Co
Spillin Mars spices across the most pristine of
*   spacescape until we war over shit that used to*
*   just come out the ground,*
till someone used what comes out the ground to
*   buy the ground.*
You know what really funded the Renaissance?

The forests.

The Atlantic Ocean.

You're wrong, Mom! Money does grow on trees.

Trees are money

We just didn't get any because Europe killed them
  to build churches after they gentrified our Savior
  and before we could get out the n———
  quarters.

I ain't salty, hell salt for sale too

Are we Finna really act like what the Standing
  Rock protesters predicted didn't happen?!

Lakota water source soiled in earth blood.

History got barz

Rhyming like a mug

If we aren't careful your next friendship will be
  another gold rush.

People as soul food

Utility

Transactional

Possessive

If you ain't careful your marriage will be just
  another gold rush.

Pleasure

Lust

Identity

It's been my findings that we seem to respond to
  crisis better than warning. And I'm not too
  confident in the first thing now.

If the vice got versed, it would body the beat
If you ain't careful, your health will be just another
  gold rush
You too busy taking advantage of you to even
  enjoy you.
Realize your quote unquote fs to give is a
  fossil fuel.
Nonrenewable
There is enough you to go around, but you need
  a code. Everything ain't for everybody.
When the last time you told someone no?
Even when the bag was oh so yes
Why is there chunks of you floating around the
  farmers and stock market?!
You couldn't bring your full self nowhere even if
  you tried
But I'll tell you what.
Dirt always wins.
Trees when they ready split sidewalks expanding
  they shoulder blades
Earth, Mars, the planet
Will be fine.
You need a break, we need each other
And though you don't owe us anything.
We all just lucky to be in your orbit.

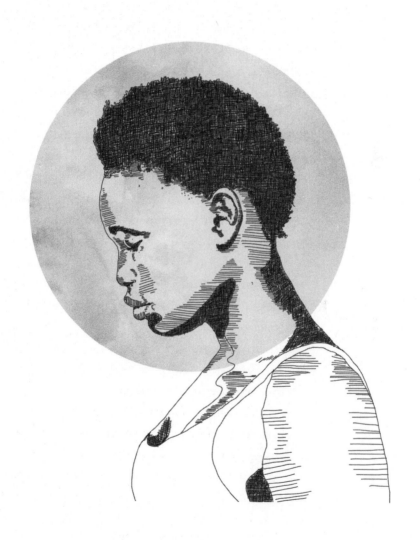

WORDS BUILD
WORLDS

The greatest prophet of our age, and you can quote me on this, is a NASCAR driver. Dead serious. He also has two first names and is fictional. He is Ricky Bobby. Ricky Bobby has so much to teach us as a people—he is the ATA terraformer! He would say things like, "If you ain't first, you're last!" He built his whole world based on this. No amount of evidence to the contrary would change his mind. The existence of his teammate Jean Girard, who was clearly a far superior driver, doesn't matter. Ricky doesn't lose! This was so completely his reality that when he crashed his car in a race, rather than admit defeat, he imagined a fire was consuming his body, which caused an imaginary paralysis of his legs. I can't stress this enough—he wasn't actually on fire, he wasn't paralyzed, he just couldn't live in a world where he wasn't first.

It's a silly example, but it does a good job of showing how in a real way, words make worlds. Not in a woo-woo way, but in a way that forms our identity. Our behavior, as well as how we see ourselves and others, is based on the stories we collectively and personally tell ourselves.

Take a nation's creation myths. When I say "myths," I don't mean is the thing true or untrue,

I mean in the sense that these are the origin stories that shape collective and individual behavior and identity. I'm going to pick on America because I'm American. Take, for example, the idea of the American dream. The American dream is, by definition, a meritocracy myth. It serves as the chief cornerstone of what it means to be an American. It means you are the master of your own destiny! You have the freedom and liberty to chart your own course and all it takes is hard work! Work hard, don't give up, and you will succeed.

And maybe for the founding fathers (who were all wealthy white men, by the way) it was this way. Well, that all sounds nice, but any fifth grader knows it's ridiculous. We all know people who have risen to levels of success who aren't the smartest, or most competent, or most deserving to be there. We all know someone whose parents are rich or connected, which helped them get to that place of power. If it was just about working hard that will lead to success, then are you telling me that the guy outside cutting the lawn ain't working hard?! The migrant farmworker? The immigrant housecleaner? I'd bet a bag of money, based on the fact that you got time to read, those other folks prolly work way harder than you! But you doin' better than them. Meritocracy ain't even a real thing in real life. Now, which one of us is gonna tell the kids that? "Honey, don't even try in school or life because it doesn't matter. I'm not connected so you will never have a better shot than this. The B-kid in your class who copies all her homework is most likely going to run the company you will work for because she's got someone on the inside to connect her."

That's not the world we want to live in. We want to believe that we do have control over our destinies, that meritocracy is real. So we tell stories about hard work, glory, and grit. It makes us . . . American. The problem is, the stories are flawed.

Build a world with bars
Like what y'all doin in Mars

As a human race, we have been terraforming the whole time. We just kept doing it by telling horrible stories. Stories of power and glory and greed and injustice. As a result, Americans are currently polarized in a way we haven't been in decades, neofascism is on the rise, and who even knows what the word *evangelical* means anymore? Even in a global—let me say it again, global crisis—that is the 2020 Covid-19 outbreak, we couldn't see our way out of the ditches we've dug ourselves into, where our position on the veracity of a virus is understood along party lines. But remember, we made up those rules! We can't blame culture. Culture is us. If we are culture, and culture is us, and we get to make it up, let's make it AMAZING.

Now, a quick note to my faith-based readers. Don't just be like, "It's sin and we need Jesus," book done. C'mon, that's lame. The prophets of our holy texts had prophetic imaginations. They cast vision, gave specifics, told creation stories, appealed to history and to the faithfulness of their God. They terraformed their world, and it was sacred work.

Can you imagine a more livable world? For real, let's build a civilization from scratch.

This book is a collection of prose, poems, and illustrations meant to spark creativity and the imagination. Let me give us the permission and the power to become terraformers ourselves, those who can reshape our homes, neighborhoods, friendships, and communities. What is preposterous but could be incredible? What is obvious but we don't even see it?! What's already here, what do we already know, what do we need, how should we treat each other? They say Imma unicorn for being interested in all this. I say striving to be fully earthling. Terraform.

There is a dark side to building a world, too. Take, for example, the Doctrine of Discovery, the document the Vatican wrote in the 1200s that gave the blessing to European explorers to basically colonize the planet and to bring "savages" under the rule of the church. It was a medieval version of a hood green light to do whatever you see fit to get a foreign land under control. There are entire tribes of people, whole civilizations, missing from the face of the earth because of this document; if the explorers killed any of them, it wasn't considered murder, because they were "savages." Boy, you can draw a straight line from there to mass incarceration, the war on drugs, George Floyd, the refugee crisis, gentrification—I could go on! That document changed Earth. Terraform!

The Doctrine of Discovery papal document, in my mind, is the perfect example of "bad storytelling" as my man Sho Baraka likes to call it. Christians of that time had an understanding of a person's origin, value, and functionality and thus built a world from that perspective. However, the world they created, for all the relative good that came about, was catastrophic to their neighbors, their fellow earthlings, who lived around the world.

I want to challenge you to tell better stories not only about yourself but about the people around you. To see the land not only as a resource, but as a family member, a gift. The very first way the Divine revealed itself. To allow your imagination

to wander into areas that you didn't even think
were possible. To build a livable world.

Imma alter your summer solstice
Imma builder of all cultures
Imma cosmic explorer
Build a new habitat
terraform.
These raps wear hard hats
Build up villages in the spots it tours at
Tsunami waves of thought demolish your old college
A new spin on things to offer you all axis
To the degree in which we lean at 23 and you.

THE CYNICAL IMAGINE

Bitterness keeps its eyes in the back of its head
Its ears to the past
Its feet in starting blocks in lieu of trigger.
Remembering all moments that destroyed sense
  of self.
Mangles taste of leftover joy.
The bitter remember.
The cynical are quite different
The cynical can taste the winds of change
Can smell the future

What of its fragrance is foul or flower
Sage or wormwood
Better or worse
Can see what we might do and what we should do
Can visualize what we could be
Yet can't,
At a guttural, moaning level
Understand why no one else can see it.
The cynical imagine
The bitter remember
I am the cynic's imagination
And source of bitterness
I don't shame either
In me contains many a paradox

MY DADDY WAS A TERRAFORMER

Honorable discharge summer 68
Pops headed straight to 41st and Central
Black Panther Watts chapter
Lemme tell you what happened after
Office got bombed by the CIA

Auntie said he came back angry
Vietnam stole his innocence
Auntie said he came back angry
What Jim Crow started it finished

What makes a man crazy?
Seeing the insides of a baby
You down to fight a war that ain't yours?
To die for a land that barely let you vote?

41st and Central his books and a pencil
Daddy was an after-school tutor
Nixon called em terrorists
So they planted their informers
Daddy was a panther
A sorta terraformer

I'M JUST AT WAR WITH MYSELF, DON'T MIND ME

Imma let you down a few times before we're
    through.
Imma say a couple things that probably really
    ain't true.
Imma sort of kind of mortify you.
Fortify you, pick a fight.
Over something silly Imma prolly lose my cool.
My excuse is
I'm a 3 with a 2 wing.
A West Coast demigod, one of many earthlings.
I'm an unfit synagogue
A one-trick silly dog
A dumb kid son of God

I done did, I been a fraud
I'm the same man that steps on stage and rain
  dance
Givens is still my main me and Eulogy still got
  same plan to step into the future
Don't let my energy fool you
I still hold only to the only holy to keep home
  from Fallujah did I lose you?
Imma Contradiction. Feel like I'm just at war
  with myself.
Imma struggling workaholic
I can't call it I can't call in sick
I can't stop it Needed 5 cups of coffee to
  accomplish this
I'm still talking to prove point ain't listenin
I built Humblebeast but my pride is still creepin
  in.
I stay trippin I blame others for my predicaments
I cut corners, I judge friends for not checking in.
I preach grace but pick and choose who still lives
  in sin
I sneak diss, then dismiss like I'm just kiddin
A grown man with 2 kids still tryin to fit in
I still long to belong that's why I'm trippin
I'm insecure, I'm fake pure. Ain't repented
My red couch is full doubt confusion

Are you smelling any notes of Genesis chapter one from the Hebrew bible? Lemme cook something for you. The creation narrative actually starts with all of creation done, it's just void of life and purpose. The story goes on to have three days of giving the universe order, separating light from dark, sky from ground, then water from dry land. Then three days of filling these things with life and purpose. Creating stars, fish, birds, animals, then finally humans. The theological argument about whether I'm supposed to read chapter one as legit surveillance camera footage or not is above my pay grade. However, it's interesting that the command God gave to humans was to be the reflection of presence in creation, to do as he did, give purpose and order. Terraform.

Martin Luther King's, The beloved city treatise:
  Terraform.
Ida B. Wells: Terraformer
The Black Panthers Ten Points program: Terraform
Black Lives Matter: Terraform
The West Virginia coal miners' union of 1921.
  They are why we have 8-hour workdays:
  Terraform
The working mother: Terraform
The coal miner,

The schoolteacher,
The firefighter,
Your OG Chola Tia and all her homegirls with
their winged eyeliner!
You, the dad who said, I am going to not be like
my dad and allow my kids to have a full range
of emotions: TERRAFORM
You, when you chose to bring your own MiiR
water flask rather than a plastic bottle:
TERRAFORM.

BIG HOMIE, TERRAFORM(?)
STILL LOST, PROP . . .

If it were possible, I would love to do one of those document searches for the frequency of a word or sentence in someone's real life. I'd be willing to bet that if Jason Petty aka Propaganda were to be run through that document search, the sentence most frequently said to him would be, "WHAT IS YOU TALKIN BOUT?!" I speak, dream, write, imagine, explain, and find joy in things that, in my assessment, can only be understood in metaphor.

I feel like some things are so true, so divine, so beautiful that words one uses to explain them, diminish them. Sometimes, the truth is greater than the words for which it's being carried. The beauty of a work of art is far more beautiful than the artwork. Like, how does one explain the intoxicating, all-consuming experience of being in love? Logically speaking, getting married, and/or having children, is literally the stupidest thing anyone could do. Your sleep? Gone! Your money? Going into someone else's mouth! Your time? Not yours anymore! Privacy?! Forget it! You will never enjoy your own meal without someone else's hand or fork invading your plate at some point. Someone will want "just a bite." You will touch or taste bodily waste multiple times! You will spend all your time, energy, and treasure trying to understand other person(s) and will fail miserably multiple times of day. Why would anyone in their right mind do such a thing?! Why? Because it's the most beautiful, fulfilling, awe-inspiring, most wonderful blissful experience.

I asked my dad, weeks before I proposed to my wife, how does one really "know" it's time or this is the "one." I remember it vividly, we were sitting on his couch, La Puente, CA, twenty minutes east of South Central, in the cool of the day. It was springtime in Los Angeles, so it was sunny and cool at about perfect degrees Fahrenheit. He started filling in some holes for me in the story of my parents' meeting, courtship, marriage, and the eventual demise of their marriage after twenty-five years. Pops, at that moment and to this day, no more than five gray hairs, still with waves that could get you seasick, who was and is currently on his fourth marriage, said, "Son, if I knew I'd write my own book and be a trillionaire! The movies are right . . . How do you know you want to be with Alma and not your last girlfriend? I don't know what to tell you. You just know. Despite any and all objections, you just know."

That answer was absolutely ridiculous, yet, somehow absolutely accurate. I was engaged once before, it didn't work out. I would never drag that young woman in public; she was a great girl and we had a lot of great times. I am a better man because of her and her family. Still, it just wasn't right, despite all signs that said the opposite. I don't think I can tell anyone what signs to look for in a lifelong partner. I don't know what needs to be seen for assurance that yo' boo thang is the perfect fit. I just know rightness about Alma was so undeniable. I can't tell you what rightness actually is, but it's kinda like . . . *insert work of art*

I got some beauty I'd like to show you. However, it's going to take an ocean of prose and a mountain of poems. You might find yourself saying, as you are working through this thing, "Wait . . . WHAT IS THIS FOO TALKIN BOUT?!" Don't worry about it, I get that often. But please, stay in the game. Don't get lost in the metaphor. I promise to do the same, nothing worse than a writer clearly writing to impress themselves. I am asking you, however, to trust me; the metaphor is the best way to show you this beauty.

LEMME DIRECT TRAFFIC
RIGHT QUICK

As promised, I'm not leaving you to navigate this terraforming process blind. I know this is a book and books have parts and chapters. But I'm a rapper so mess with me on this. I see terraforming in a series of movements. And the chapters each fit in these movements. If that's confusing, think of it in terms of acts and scenes like plays. And if you heard the *Terraform* album, the following titles of the parts in this book will be familiar.

The Sky—We have all we need!

While I was in Israel, I learned about a farming philosophy in the region. It's based on the local tribal belief that God made creation in perfect balance, so for every issue, there is a solution in nature. For example, if a farmer has a worm problem, and the worm population is kept in check by rats, maybe there are too many rats, which leads to the falcons who eat the rats. Nature has what it needs, and so do we. The sky is a symbol of the magic of the universe: it already contains in it all that is necessary for human life. All of us already have all we need. This theme is found in this part's chapters, "Tell Better Origin Stories" and "The Truth Is Yelling at You."

The Soil—*The soil is sacred.*

Sometimes I wonder, if trees produced Wi-Fi, would we treat them better? Too bad they only produce food and oxygen! Have you ever stopped to think about how the ground has not only given you all the food and drink you and every living creature has ever consumed, it is also the building block of every person you have ever loved? We did nothing to make that happen, it just is. The soil is such a gift. Sacred. You got no life if you got no soil. We should act as if we understand that life comes from the soil. Because it does. This theme is in this part's "Soil Is Sacred" chapter.

The People—*We are all we got.*

We talked about this some in this chapter already, but I always giggle when people talk about culture like it's a living thing separate from us. Like it's a monster that lives in the mountains, feeding on our children, taking prayer out of our schools, creating homosexuality, and ruining the economy. Culture is just a term we use to understand how two or more humans plan to survive. How we communicate, how we treat each other, and how we understand the world around us. No humans, no culture. We can't be at war with the culture, we are the culture. We can't save the culture, we are the culture. We are who we are looking for, we are who we needed. If you have a desire to see the treatment of others improve, learn this, you are the other, and the other is also you, the culture is us. We made it up. So if we get to make it up, let's make it amazing. This theme is explored in this part's chapters, "Institutional Neighborliness" and "Remember the Quiet."

The Possibility—Imagine a better future.

It's a little difficult to notice, but we are sitting in the shadow of the past. Some events cast such a large shadow that it's near impossible to fathom anything different, anything before. We sit in the shadow of the Age of Discovery, so colonialism is just a fact. We sit in the shadow of Enlightenment, so rationalism and empiricism is just how knowledge works. We still sit in the shadow of Chattel Slavery, so institutionalized racism is just a fact. But these facts were not always facts. Just like we made culture, so we humans created and defined these ideas. Democrat or Republican, conservative or liberal, these don't HAVE to be your only choice. America doesn't have to have more humans in prison than any other country. You don't HAVE to see yourself the way you do. Instead, have some prophetic imagination. What could we be? If we could start from scratch, how should we build the future? What beautiful new way could it look and operate? These themes are in the last chapter, "Imagine a Better Future."

START OVER

Lord Jesus let the soil teach us,
And maybe value trees like they give us the air we
    breathe.
I have no truer words to speak or not
But I'm pretty positive that the Equinox is screaming
    about beef we got!
Start over.
Why do we even bother to try to solve problems
When in 30 years WE'LL BE OUT OF FRESH WATER
Overdue for a do-over.
Empires rise and fall
Terraform
Start over
Be better for us all.

WHAT WE MADE WE CAN'T SUSTAIN

Our passion
Our Temper, love and our anger
We know nothing save life in red zone, Danger
What we made we can't sustain
What we made we can't maintain
Our love conversation topics
Our urges so toxic
What we made we can't sustain
Appetite ferocious love devours each other
We are binary stars
We felt the full force of each other's gravity
And we danced.
As Shiva's dance of destruction we danced
And our attraction
We drew the stars nigh, they surrounded us.
    Orbiting our heart's apartments
Stayed glued to our pull.
We were moons to each other's oceans,
We regulate our tides.
Yet the warning signs of a developing quasar was
    way-far,
We just danced.
And dined.
And gorged.
We ain't see the DJ was closing his laptop. Club
    Space Love was flickering its warning lights.

We consumed each other
Without an ounce of regard for anyone's life
    including ours,
We made what we can't sustain.
We built a life on the assumption that all will
    always run hot.
Astronomy teaches,
The vast majority of lights in tonight's sky,
    burned out around the Iron Age. It just takes
    light that long for its vibes to reach us,
We are living in the past right now.
We danced under its ancient light not knowing it
    was over before it started.
Star currently collapsed on itself.
Could not withstand the weight of its own
    creation.
Crushed by its own forces.
Self-actualizing cause and effect now nothing can
    escape, not even itself.
What we made we can't sustain.
We could see each other under it but couldn't see
    ourselves in it, we are it.
We are twin black holes in the center of self-
    centeredness—the galaxy of me
We drew many worlds to us yet
We've collapsed a long time ago.
We, all of Western civ have gone the way of
    Babylon and we ain't even know it.

We are the world we built
We are the violence and the beauty
We are the hope and destruction
We are keepers and destroyers of culture and
*   planet*
We are grave fillers and robbers
Death by ignorance
Blissful b lines into the northern sea iceberg
Dance magic dance, band keep playing
We are binary stars destined to rip each other
*   asunder*
What we made we can't sustain.
What we made we can't maintain.

You gon alter the summer solstice
You a builder of new cultures
You a cosmic explorer
Build a new world
Big homie, terraform.

TERRAFORMING
PROJECT 1

I'm going to close every chapter with one or more short tasks and exercises to help you put into practice building a livable world.

This first step will get your creative juices going.

Most likely adulthood has ruined your imagination: what *is* has fogged your ability to think of what *could be*. The final chapter will have us creating what could be. But to start, we need to get loose. This is sketchbook time. The sky's the limit! We are making a planet, a culture from scratch!

I. MAKE A LIST OF WHAT'S NORMAL.
Make a list of things that, in your view, our world has normalized that maybe shouldn't be normal! What things make you say, "it doesn't have to be this way!"? For me, the first thing I think of is partisan politics! The terms "left" and "right" come from the French Revolution, based on which sides of the room each party sat on! We don't have to think of the government this way. It doesn't have to be this way.

What would the government look like? What would the church look like? What would families look like? More egalitarian? More giving? Small government? Big government? What would your democracy look like? Like our democracy? More socialist? Maybe all these words and categories fall short completely. You tell me.

Save this list because we are gonna come back to it at the end of the book.

THE SKY

TELL BETTER ORIGIN STORIES

We are our stories
So, tell better stories

A BETTER ORIGIN STORY

The banjo is from West Africa
Appalachia used to be filled with runaway slaves
That's why folk music has banjos
Yup, we made that music too
The end.

Let me tell you a story.

I was standing with DJ Efechto, Victoria Hernandez, my wife, Alma, our two kids, and my dawg Corey Paul on an Apache rez in Arizona. We were there to do a show. We played some basketball with the little homies, had some fry bread, and listened to music. For those who have never been on a rez, the site might be very difficult to picture. Some reservations, depending on location and tribal gaming money, are some of the most picturesque landscapes of rolling hills and wildlife, while others look like a mix between a dirty South project and a trailer park in the middle of the most inhospitable, unfarmable land our continent has to offer. One thing that they all have in common is . . . the people who live there don't own the land. One time, according to my Apache homies, the government messed up and sold land rights to a tribe that discovered oil under their soil; they said it was an Oklahoma tribe, I think. Now that tribe owns the rights.[1] Tio Sam doesn't make the same mistake twice.

Native Americans are as diverse as any other people group. Depending on region, climate, and norms, their myths, legends, creation stories, and dances can be as different from each other as Jackson, Mississippi, is from Berkeley, California.

We walked out to a monument, about a mile off the paved road. It was honoring those who fell in the death march to the land they now live on. I remembered a trip I took a few years back to the Crow Nation rez and how they talked about the four corners of the wind and how the world was made, so I asked if the Apache had a creation story.

"Well, I think somewhere in those caves out there are some cave writings about our creation. I could take you over there but that's written history, and oral history is more trustworthy so . . ." my friend told me.

That sentence stopped time. Did he just say oral was more trustworthy than written?! My insides shouted in the collective accent of the Enlightenment and all Western civilization, "I'M

CONFUSED, BIG FELLA!" This goes against all my theological and academic training. As I sat with the statement, I thought to myself, *Well, you know, the Bible is oral history.* Every character of the Old Testament relied on oral history, friggin Passover, the Shabbat, is oral history. Aren't the holy texts just oral stories that got written down a ton of years later?

Yo! When I was a kid and my grandma, on various occasions, asked what I was learning at school, sometimes she would say in her perfect southern drawl, "Oh baby they don't know what they talkin 'bout, I was there, this what happened." I would wholeheartedly believe my grandma and her experiences over any and all textbooks. I have no desire to make a hard-and-fast rule, or create some sort of a false dichotomy; what if the truths you spoke over your friends and family were more set in stone than what is actually set in stone?

Want to hear an even crazier thought? That's already how you live.

TRUE, GOOD, AND BEAUTIFUL STORIES

I'm aware that when you hear the word *story* you might associate it with the idea of truth. We often ask if a story is true or fable. I think that's the wrong question, though. Let me give you a history lesson. Before the Enlightenment . . . Then because of the Enlightenment, when we say "true" we mean in an empirical sense. Can we measure or verify the factualness of something? For our purposes, the facts of the narrative are not really the point. For example, have you ever tried to recount a significant event, and as you're working through the story, you skip over a few parts or don't focus on other parts for the purpose of getting to the point. However your buddy keeps correcting you, like, "Naw, bro, that wasn't how it happened, it wasn't Sunday, it was Tuesday!" or " Naw, dude, your shirt was blue, not red!" It's not that your buddy is incorrect, it's just not the point you were trying to make.

When I say stories, I mean what does a story invoke in a person that brings forward the humanity necessary for a more livable world? I am not saying lying is fine as long as it makes you a better person, because I'm not sure a lie can even do that. Make no mistake, truth is beautiful, I'm not here to sanitize your past. I am saying that the beauty of a good story is that it draws out the beauty in us. Our focus is how the stories we tell make us who we are. So let's take a look at the stories we are telling.

My superpower is self-awareness. I have the un-canny ability to keep it very real with myself. So, guys, let's be real with each other. We all believe something that explains the world, and we turn this into our foundational stories, and if you think about it, you'll see that these things are absolutely ridiculous. Whether it's God, virgin birth, the universe, positive energy, crystals, sage, ancestors, incantations, or fatalism, if you adjust the camera lens out far enough, they become almost laugh-able. We're the youngest species on a planet that's not even the center of the solar system, spinning around a star that's not even noticeable in a ran-dom galaxy that's just one of innumerable galaxies. Even consciousness is kinda preposterous. Why does this version of hairless animal know it's a hairless animal? Why did this ape and not those antelopes grow a prefrontal cortex? When the aliens come and observe this planet they accidentally found, they will see one of the hairless apes, aka a human, make a certain noise (some sort of insult) to another hairless ape, then they fight and make explosions! That's so weird.

When people say "the universe" as if it has per-sonhood, I'm always like, okay, what part do you mean?! Quasars? Dark matter? Spiral quarks? The universe is literally everything so you said nothing. However, if I'm being a hunnid, which again is my superpower, I do know what they mean; they mean the collective forces that seem to govern how nature and physics works surely must govern over these particular apes that know they are apes on this random-ass rock.

I got homies that keep crystals in their house to channel vibrations. Since sounds are just vibrating atoms, I suppose it wouldn't be too far of a jump to think that since my brain and body are just atoms that the crystal would have an effect on me.

I suppose it's not too far of a jump to be sure there must be a benevolent being out there seeing as how there's really no reason for the universe to have living beings at all, let alone living beings that are experiencing themselves. Especially when the rest of the cosmos is so unfathomably big. I mean there are stardust clouds that are five light-years long. You know how big you gotta be to not be measured by meters or miles but in TIME?! There has got to be a "why" for the fact that we know that we are here.

Self-awareness makes graciousness. Ain't we all just trying to make sense out of chaos? Ain't we all just spinning on this rock?! Ain't we all just hairless apes that know we're hairless apes? Ain't we all just looking for meaning?! Weren't ancient Greeks arguing over which god was pulling the sun across the sky? Sounds silly to you? Not to them, so I wonder which modern debates will sound silly in a thousand years? I don't really understand what life even is. I don't really understand life's origins or its purpose. Does that make life any less beautiful?

IS IT ANY LESS BEAUTIFUL?

Is it any less beautiful?
Even if it is symbolic,
Is it any less beautiful?
Whether real or metaphor,
Is it any less beautiful?
Broken legs or broken hearts
And by hearts, you mean atrium?
Or ventricles?
Broken as in artery rupture
Or broken as in the plaque buildup of unrequited
openness.
When vulnerability is punished
When bruised reed of a backbone is crushed by
negligence or repulse
Broken nonetheless
Whether heart actually skips beat
Or you really swallowed caterpillars
they survived their cocooning
to never venture out of digestive tract,
to only flutter when crush passes.

Whether love is felt in soul or tummy.
Bravery in intestines.
No one says I love you with all my kidneys.
But does not your soul burn within you?
Are you any less beautiful?
What is Love
or Belief?
or forgiveness
But chemical reactions in our bodies,
The morning commute of atoms and enzymes,
glands poppin off at the mouth and pulsating it
    through your body.
It's just chemicals.
Are you any less in love?
Whether Divine, choosing to self-limit and
Co-laboring with creation,
choosing to include us in its own identity.
Hand stitching
Sewing up sinews
Or processes far above what our antennas have
    been attuned to
Over billions of eons
Random is a matter of perspective
Whether true or communicating truths
Whether factual or wisdom
Wooden or whimsy
Whether Emmanuel or Kant
We are

self-aware
We are special
Are you any less beautiful?

BAD STORIES DESTROY

If you are in any way like me, I imagine most of your self-destructive thoughts and actions come from you telling yourself a bad story about yourself. I don't think we as individuals, and for damn sure collectively, really have a grasp on how much the way we see ourselves really comes from the origin stories we tell. I know this is how racism works. Our nation told itself that natives were savages and Africans were inferior so genocide and enslavement doesn't really count when it's enacted on either of these peoples. It scares me to death when I begin to notice how much of that I believed about myself. When all the sound is turned off, I can hear the tiny germ holding a mic in my brain affirming that crime in the inner city or financial struggle really is because something is just wrong with my people. Unbeknownst to me, I internalized an origin story.

This is partly because as a nation, we have gone out of our way to try to convince ourselves that we are a pure meritocracy knowing full well we are not and never have been. Some of the most crippling moments of inaction and self-doubt in my own life, both personally and professionally, didn't stem from outside pressures, but from the thing I told myself about who I am and how far I could go in this world. I didn't realize Jason personally was telling himself he only came from suffering. This cognitive dissonance that despite all the Black boy/girl magic we have shown we can pull off, Black people can only make it so far. But if I just work harder, I'll win.

I, we, all of us, must tell a better story than this. We cannot be afraid to venture into this process. We have to look honestly at what we've become due to these bad stories. America has been telling itself that it's the greatest country in the world despite not having a single statistic that supports that claim. We are too afraid to look at our origin story to understand that we were birthed out of violence, we celebrate violence, and we amassed our wealth off the back of slave labor, all on land we stole. And to this day, we have never made these things right. Telling a better origin story is not about forgetting the past but being willing to look at the past in all its destruction and glory, see how it crippled who we are now, but also how a retelling can forge a better person, a better nation. Let me tell you some better stories.

BETTER COLLECTIVE
ORIGIN STORY

CHAOS IS CANVAS

The most colorful concoction of ink splatters
of family matters
A combination of mystical
logical
historical
transcendent,
None of this makes sense
Yet the only thing that does is that all things
   return to it.
Chaos
the idea that identities at the slightest gust of
   winds, swing as a pendant
The idea that culture is a construct
concocted from our consciousness.
This was all our making,
Making form from puffs of smoke
Forming something that is doing its best to run
   back to its natural state
Chaos
our synapses are onto us
What does God offer us?
An incessant need to know?
What difference will it make?

What difference do I make?
A brain taking in scenes and converting them into
    meaning
Landmarks of self-evidence,
The Chaos is canvas.
A beautiful brush fire.
As death screams to life you can have it!
Wilderness just as untamed as it is ordered.
Life making chaotic, orchestrated oracles
Can someone explain to chlorophyll that it is weird
    and shouldn't even be a thing?
What in the hell is a jellyfish?! Nervous system
    with tentacles?
Chaos!
Nonsense
Don't all of this seem preposterous?!
Am I trippin?
Cacophony and symphony in the hands of God
    is samsies
the strangest of bedfellows
Chaos and harmony
Quite a primordial soup
You and me seem to be from
Chaos,
It must be canvas

There are two types of stories: personal and collective. Personal stories are the ones about our own lives—such as, here's what has happened in the forty years I've been alive. Collective stories are about a people group. Any community you are a part of has a story, a history; for example, as Americans, when we tell stories about our shared history, that's the collective story.

Back on the Apache reservation, I was smashing my fourth fry bread with nopales, a decision I deeply regretted later. That gluten got in my belly and stretched its wings out like this whole space belongs to him. Being the woke artist I am, I asked about fry bread and why so many tribes eat it. I thought maybe I would get some sort of "shared ancestor" story that you would have to be a part of the culture to know. Big homie responded with the most pan face expression. An expression I've seen before in the face of Black and brown kids in the projects while explaining the most wild stuff, as if trauma erases microexpressions.

"Naw, when our people were captured, the ones that weren't killed were marched to wherever the army said would be our land and given a ration of flour and oil for food. We just figured out that we should fry it. And the nopales (Spanish word for cactus) was just the only plant available in the desert."

I now can empathize with white people when they ask Black people questions that the answer to is "because of slavery." The origin of fry bread is oppression. At that moment I felt so connected to him. I've been on his side of a question like this. Though we are from two different backgrounds, we both understand the collective story of being an oppressed people group. We also know what it means to make treasure out of trash. Frying up flour in oil for the Native Americans, or hot links, chitterlings, pig feet, fat back, neck bones, black-eyed peas, catfish, snapper, and shrimp for the African Americans. Soul food, trash the massa was throwing out, my ancestors made gourmet!

One of the things I'm most proud of about Black Americana is our ability to make something out of nothing. Knowing the food that was allotted was trash according to the standard of those that meant to enslave you, is now not only nourishing you, but is the envy of the oppressors' descendants. Man, y'all WISH you could cook like Madea! And thus goes the story about fry bread, it's the same story as chitterlings. It's trash. Because our oppressors saw us as less important than their pets, they fed this trash to us.

Here's our better origin story: Sitting in your bones, and on your plate, is proof that you can make treasure and vitality out of anything. That's where we come from. That's what's on your plate doused with Red Rooster hot sauce. Our food is testament to our ancestral land. We make something from nothing. We survive. We overcome.

A BETTER ORIGIN STORY

Coffee was discovered in Ethiopia
Yah we gave y'all coffee too
The end.

CUP OF NOODLES AND HOT LINKS

Lil homie nothing did the trick
Homie let me learn you trick
Black people teach ya how to breathe it tho.
Exnihilo somethin out of nothin you should see
    it tho.
Black boy joy
Black boy fly
Black girl rock
Hit a rock make it cry
We hold the staff of Moses can't call it,
It's magic,
Learned from ten thousand hours of not having it.
A couple cups of noodles and hot links

Gourmet feast.
A miracle nothing short of trees sprouting from
*   concrete.*
Right out of concrete.
Cracking the concrete.
Y'all are beyond weak.

BETTER PERSONAL
ORIGIN STORY

The Apaches taught me to remember to tell a better collective origin story. My close friends and family have shown me the importance of telling a better personal origin story. A personal origin story has more to do with your own history and the people that have directly affected you. Although it's impossible to separate the personal from the collective, it is important to do so in order to understand yourself better. These personal origin stories often stem from family interactions, school experiences, friendships, and lovers. Like it or not, we are not closed off from one another. These people and events shape the language and tenor of our self-talk. The tone of your inside voice, whether it's judgmental or very nurturing, comes from your past. Maybe you're telling a story of your fuckup tendencies, maybe you never felt like

you belonged, maybe you're gonna always have to strive for love. The stories come in all colors and shapes. They can be loud and obnoxious or sly and slick. Either way, I think it's high time we take them to task.

But I want to take a minute to recognize that for many people, this is easier said than done. It's not my story to tell, but at least five people in my closest circle of friends and family have endured some sort of abuse. Whether psychological, physical, emotional, or sexual, the abuse they endured was at levels too brutal for words. Some of my folks have for their whole life dealt with serious abandonment issues that would fold in two the strongest of backbones. I know firsthand what the effects of good meds, a ton of therapy, a ton of prayer, meditation, and constant grace from the rest of us can do.

LET ME TELL YOU WHAT I'M NOT GON' DO

I'm not going to tell you that telling yourself a better story about your abuse will make the pain go away and somehow right that wrong. Naw fam. It's wrong what happened to them, to you. It's ugly and unfair and disgusting, and you have every right to every emotion you experience. Telling a better story is not erasure! It's looking back and seeing if there is another narrative you can rehearse that brings life out of the suffering. I tell you what, people who have been through this kind of abuse and somehow get the help they need see the world, see people's suffering, with such grace and love. I marvel at it. Those people who have been working through this stuff, you possess a superpower!

LET ME TELL YOU WHAT I'M NOT GON' DO

I'm not going to say that any of those things, or anything in this book, is a magic pill. Healing isn't like breaking a bone where simply putting a cast on does the trick. The breaks I'm talking about don't work that way. Healing means more of a change of norms, integrating healthier practices. Healing means creating new neurological pathways. Some of the damage caused by abuse shows up in your actual biology. In which case, meds are the way to go! I have homies with PTSD, some from war overseas and some from war in the streets. When my wife was in a deep depression, I thought she just needed a finite amount of therapy sessions to fix her. I learned it's not about fixing; it's about health. You don't just go to the gym once and work out like a boss then be like, welp, I'm healthy! Glad that's done! Take the time you need, take the medications you need, take the help you need to take care of yourself.

LET ME TELL YOU WHAT
I'M NOT GON' DO

I'm not gonna tell you your pain is a usable commodity for the rest of society! It's up to you what you do with your healing. But I will say this, should you choose to tell your better story, it will transform you into a terraformer of the worlds of your listeners. You just gave a person's planet their first taste of breathable air.

LET ME TELL YOU WHAT
I'M NOT GON' DO

I'm not going to tell you that you need to hunt for some sort of divine plan or purpose for your suffering. Some things are just worthy of lament. There is an entire book of the Bible called Lamentations. Its lesson: This sucks! All of it! Sucks! Maybe there is a divine lesson being cooked up, I guess it mostly depends on where you think the story stops. What seems like the end might just be the second act. I do hold to a C. S. Lewis view of God: not safe, but good.

A BETTER ORIGIN STORY

Chocolate came from
Pre-Columbian Mezo-America
Found in what is modern-day
Honduras in 1400 BC
On behalf of all humans
Gracias ancient Honduras
The end.

OVERHEARD IN CERRITOS

Overheard a group of 20-somethings arguing over
The worthiness of mourning
Apparently one must earn grief
The subject: XXXTentacion
Insert Young Purp, Peep
Or any other lil
As if life choices are as fixed and as simple as a
    two-party political system
Nuance free, flatten it all.
Such an unwashed mirror of culture
Funhouse distorting concept of human dignity.
Same energy fuels immigration rhetoric
What in the actual is a good immigrant?
As if they are crops that either edible or fertilizer

I've been terrorized by MS-13.
Never crossed my mind that they were not human.
What is gangster but lost boys just like my cousins
  who shot back at them.
Longing for belonging
Humanity makes us accountable.
When stripped,
it crumbles the very mountain of righteousness you
  stand on.
Such binary make cowards of us all
And such naïve hue of resolution drips with
  contradictions
So BURN HIS ASHES or WHO CARES
  WHAT LIFE WAS LED WHEN LIFE
  IS LOST?!
We are doomed if these are our only choices.
Death doesn't erase
But death still sucks.
Is there a grand story?
I don't know, I haven't seen the last chapter

A BETTER ORIGIN STORY

The Beatles,
Mick Jagger,
Billy Preston all opened for,
Jimi Hendrix played guitar for
And James Brown sang background for
Little Richard
Yup we made rock music too
The end.

BETTER STORIES
MAKE BETTER PEOPLE

Deep sighs. Breathe, Prop. "What is you cryin for?"! *Lord, why did you give me daughters?!*

This is my self-talk. Being a girl dad has its privileges. I find myself in conversations, saying sentences, and being made privy to information that never in my wildest dreams would I have ever thought I'd be a part of. Some of what I've learned I wouldn't wish on my worst enemy, others have undoubtedly made me a better man, better person. I don't always see these moments as gifts though. So buckle up, my daughter is about to show me how better stories make better people. I need you to feel what I felt tho, so I gotta set the scene.

It's summertime in Los Angeles in the Alma-ganda home. Where bedtimes and screen time are just a suggestion, and we never really change out of our beach clothes. Tomorrow, however, we have a trip planned. I can't remember what the desti-nation was but I knew bedtime must be enforced. You might think that once you leave the toddler stage that getting your child to go to bed would become easier. I'm here to report that that is not the case. Alma and I have gone to great lengths to figure out how to get our teen to finally go to sleep. One rule is the phone charging station: we don't have phone chargers in our rooms, they are in the living room, and we expect to see all phones plugged in at a certain time in the living room.

On this particular night, it's about 11:30 p.m. and it's time to go enforce this rule. In full dad regalia, shirtless, shoeless, holding the leftover ice from a cocktail, I approach my daughter's room. In full teen girl regalia and all its splendor, messy bun, short shorts, sports bra, my child responds, "Okay" and walks to plug in her precious iPhone. I noticed something in the way she said "okay." It's that type of way that sounds like she is holding back some-thing. I see a river of tears flowing from her eyes as she attempts to not make eye contact with me.

Here's something you need to know about me—I've always believed tears were the final expression of emotions, what comes when you've reached your capacity to handle the moment. It's the ultimate expression of your wits' end. I don't know where I got that belief from. Maybe it has to do with the playground policing boys do as we figure out our masculinity. If you are crying that means something is serious. You don't cry if it's not that bad.

I often believe that tears are used as a tool of manipulation. I'm currently unlearning that so bear with me. If my daughter or wife is crying—especially over something that, in my assessment, isn't even that serious—I feel like they're forcing me to stop. If we are in a discussion and I'm trying to make a point but my wife is breaking into tears, then that means I've gone too far and I've hurt her. Which gets me riled up because she is crying, which means I have to stop talking. Again, I don't know where I got that from. Somehow I've convinced myself that everyone has this scale in their head of how to demonstrate their level of culpability with emotions.

Watching my daughter in this moment, tears in her eyes, it might be hard to appreciate the vast conflicting emotions that come over a father. A high percentage of your mind has deep concern for your child's well-being. The protector in you kicks in and you want to destroy whatever caused her suffering. There's a smaller percentage of you that has to try to remember that you can't just be a hammer. Sometimes you gotta be a consoler, so you think to yourself, *What would Mom do?* And it's not so much that Mom knows how to do this by virtue of her nature, my wife is from the streets. It's not at all her nature to be nurturing. She has just as much "suck it up" energy in her vibe as I do in mine. But since my daughter sees my wife as the sole provider of emotional support, she has a lot of practice in just rubbing backs and self-love mantras. I'm exhausted just describing it. Then there's the largest percentage of you that draws from a deep well of what might be a toxic masculine version of how to deal with pain. The truest feeling I have as a dad at this moment is in-convenienced. It's terrible but it's true. No father of the year awards for me if the criteria includes my thought life, too. I'm thinking about how this two-minute trip to her room is now about to be an hour-and-a-half process of me suppressing my irritation and becoming a better human. No part of me is excited about growing right now. I just want to go to bed. Why. is. this. girl. always. crying?! What is it now?! Some friend didn't text you back?! Some boy made fun of your forehead?! Tuffin up! Thicken your skin! WHY do I have to have only girls?! I know, I'm terrible.

Thankfully, my higher self responded.

"Baby, are you good? Can I help in any way?"

She says no and runs to Mom!

Cool! I'm off the hook!

Just kidding. I'm actually bummed that my kid doesn't find me safe for her emotions. . . . I'll go make another cocktail.

Forty-five minutes later my daughter and wife exit the bedroom. They both explain to me what the tears were about. Y'all ready?

Stranger Things season 3.

Blink blink.

The Netflix series.

Yeah.

Two weeks before we had binged season three. I'm not going to spoil it if you haven't seen it, but the final episode just absolutely broke my daughter. "For real, *Stranger Things*? The TV show? That we watched two weeks ago?" This one thing has got me trippin'—we watched it two weeks ago. Why is she crying about it tonight?

"You are at your complete emotional end, over fictional characters?!" This is my inside voice, thank the Lord.

"Oh, that's it? Baby, it's not real. It's just a show. Stop crying, go to bed! Problem solved." Is what I wanted to say.

What she taught me is that she wasn't crying

over imaginary characters. She was crying over the truth. Here's what I know about good storytelling—the truth it's communicating is greater than the words it's being carried by. Here's another example: you can ask yourself, Is the Bible true or is it communicating truth? I don't know which hill you want to die on but I think dying on one of those hills is missing the point. Is Genesis 1 about how the earth was made? All 'bout putting the atoms together to form the universe? I doubt it because remember, the universe was already completed at the beginning of Genesis 1. Go read it again. Or is Genesis 1 communicating something greater than the facts of the story? Is it saying that all things have purpose, beauty, identity, and function? All things have order and design? All things display a goodness far beyond our imagination? I don't know, you tell me.

My daughter is crying over the deep feelings of human connection like friendship and love, bonds that are so much greater than blood ties. That going through things together and finding the bravery to be a different person than you were in the beginning is something worth celebrating. That mourning the loss of someone who's important to you without being able to say how you truly feel about that person is deeply devastating. I'm proud of my daughter. She saw more than a multimillion-dollar series; she saw the greater truth, the greater beauty, which is so much more beautiful, which is so much more true. A higher story than the Upside Down could ever be. She's telling a way better story than I was. She merged the better collective story with the better individual story and that made her a better person whose empathy will help build a more livable world.

Looks like I learned something new after all. I think I'll make another cocktail.

LET THE ORIGIN ANSWER

When they ask who you are, next time let me
  answer.
I'll give a dose of poetry with the potency of
  dopamine
I will name drop a level that would shame every
  rap the Game rocked
I will pull out some obscure reference to trigger
  insecurity in the vein of
Oh you ain't heard that band?
Or oh you want sugar and cream for your coffee?
Or you never read that book?
Hmm.
I will unroll a scroll of receipts and flexes
In the vein of Game of Thrones introductions

Imma light up the lineage living in your double
   helixes
Scream
YAS QUEEN!
GO OFF!
HE DON'T MISS!
QUIT PLAYIN WITH HER!
RESPECK ON IT!
ON MOMAS!
ON PERIODT!
And whatever y'all say now that means what
   those are
Imma gas you the fuckup!
Let me answer next time!
When they ask where you are,
When you found out the man that introduced
   moms to Jesus died, at the very moment
   your gleeful 4-year-old came bouncing in from
   playtime looking for snacks
Fully immersed in the present
Beckoning you join her in her innocence
This has to be the most disorienting version of
   now.
One moment, the same moment
Pulling you to your past and future.
What is even time?
Breakups on birthdays.
Depressed while Black.

Comment section wars under the most beautiful of
sunsets.
When it feels like open roads and flat plains and
your brain can't grab it.
A 360 horizon line, how a round is flat?
The gravitas tugs and fights and makes it make
sense
When you forget the hard-fought deaths to allow
you margins to even ponder.
Next time they ask where you are, let me answer
When they ask why you are, let me answer
Imma point at moments
Mountains
Movies
Novels
Day cares
Imma scream into the future,
When you become the object of flex
When you are the receipt I roll out the day your
descendants
Are asked these very questions
Imma holler GOT THIS!
Let me answer!
I got a story for you

A BETTER ORIGIN STORY

At the very least, 5,000 years ago
And lowkey on accident,
Emperor Shen Nung of China discovered tea when
    leaves from
a wild tree blew into his pot of boiling water.
The end.

TERRAFORMING
PROJECT 2

Fair warning. All these tasks might be triggering
so be careful. My hope, however, is that it turns
into healing and better self-talk.

1. FIND OUT WHERE YOU'RE FROM.
   If there are any elders in your family around,
   ask them some questions. Find out about
   where they are from. If this is not an option
   due to drama, trauma, or death, maybe
   find a family friend or cousin. I'm positive
   there is a survivor in your bones. Try to find
   it. If you can't find it in your family, find
   it in your land of origin. You come from
   amazing stock. Go digging.

2. **WRITE A LOVE POEM TO YOUR NEIGHBORHOOD.** If those memories are ugly and painful, maybe getting it all on paper will bring up a lot of hurt. I know it did for me. But after a while, I started seeing beauty. Maybe it's time to revise that history. Maybe there's a better story in there, kinda like fry bread and chitterlings.

3. **TRACE YOUR OWN BODY FOR SCARS.** Take a second to remember how you got them, then tell yourself what a scar means. A scar means you've healed, you survived. You made it.

4. **WRITE YOUR OWN "TELL ME YOURS."** On my 2014 album *Crimson Cord*, the record ends with a poem that shouts out all the names and places that made me who I am. Good and bad. It was one of the most healing things I've done. Maybe you just write a list, it doesn't have to be as poetic as mine, but again, getting out of your head might train you to see your origins as beautifully as I see them. Here is mine:

I'm honestly not looking for "thank yous" because
I don't deserve them. I didn't earn um.

But you can thank South Central.
The San Gabriel Valley. Run up PCH to East
   Bay and thank Lake Merritt.
Every Turf Walker and scraper bike. When ya see
   one, say thanks for Prop's music.
Posyden, who made sure the bar was high in the
   cypher.
Krystal Kevin Corey, the other Black family in
   Valinda.
Thomas Pokinghorn. He's why I even liked rap.
Thank the I.E., Foundation, the hardest battles
   I've ever been in against Triune, Dead-Eye, or
   Ishues
The Breuman, Zaragosa, Wilbur family
   introduced me to the gospel.
Reynosa, Coleman, Whitenhill, Robles tribe, My
   Sri Lankan twin Holden.
Ronnie David Robles. He's the first to put a
   spray can in my hand and my imagination
   expanded. Why my art is ambidextrous.
I owe you one, hermano. Trujillo, Montez, Sales,
   Carrasco. Told I grew up with the vatos!
Leon, Myron, Junie, Mrs. Venita Shells, Uncle
   Ray, Aunt Fannie Mae, Vakaa Rose and
   Aunt Ethell
Mr. Jeffery, Mrs. Cronan, Mr. Paliki who came
   to get me when I was ditching US history,
   trying to keep up with Trevor Pennick.

*Thank David Utley. He told me he thought God
made Black people by smearing them with
feces. And Brad Sutton, who called rap jungle
jive! True story! That's what drove me to the
scriptures and years later offered yal Lofty.*

*Dr. Anderson, David Rojas, Mr. Singer, Doug
Thigpen. Mrs. Monje and Herrera for turning
down my advances.*

*lol! Would have never met mi Alma. Thank
Silivana, Miss Jenna Kamp.*

*The most outside-the-box teachers that knew these
kids could learn at risk didn't buy that at-risk
rhetoric. Nicolette. The Wilsons.*

*An adopted clan of 12. I witnessed troubled
abandoned kids get loved into success!*

*Huizars, Neyda. Dahlia and Graciella Conchas.
I was there when your pop died. I still got
that bracelet. Cynthia Saldana Oh! Patience
and both Uplands. Tiffany, Kaamill, Spencer
Masonry, Bianca, Uyen, Nick Luvano, and
Raphi Cala. These kids were the fuel for at
least three albums.*

*Thank the Blowed. Thank Mic and Dim Lights,
up the street round the corner where my heart is
best kept.*

*Thank Best Kept and Shihan. They are why I
love poetry. And the encouragement of my Ate,
Irene Fay Duller, who said to try my hand*

at poetry. How's Jodel doin?! Thank El Taco
Nazo. Where Taboo of the Black Eyed
Peas accidentally kicked me and chipped my
front tooth.
True story
Thank Zane One and Sareem poems and Ozay
Moore.
Rosario Ortega, Shames Worthy
James, Janice, Nichole Petty
Thomas Joseph Terry
These deserve your thanks.
If you see them tell them I sent you.
I didn't know it then but now I can't ignore.
This is my crimson cord.
Tell me yours?

PLOT TWIST

This poem was one of the, if not *the*, most ther-
apeutic pieces of art I've ever done. As a matter
of fact, it marked the beginning of my own pro-
cess of healing and therapy. Of getting healthy. Of
when I began to tell a better origin story.

Now, I'm a bunch of years away from 2013. I
see that I missed a few strands in my crimson cord.
Funny thing about health, it's not a "one and done"
type thing. Time marches on, life keeps moving.

Memory is an active and living thing. New events pop up and that causes us to grow. It forced me to retell some past stories too. Turns out my origin story is still being shaped. There are people, places, events that I forgot about. Things I once thought were mundane turned out to be earth moving. It's a lesson I wouldn't see until many years later. New people, who were at the time just acquaintances, become deep long-lasting friends. Their love could make you realize that your last best friend may have actually been kinda shitty to you. History revised. New people take residence in your heart. Your origin story is truly still active. Keep telling it. Revisiting chapters, polishing off varnish, reveals beauty we had no idea was there. So in the spirit of this, I'm gonna participate with you rewriting a new "tell me yours." Here it is:

TELL ME AGAIN

I'm sorry I forgot you
I don't deserve you, but thank you
I forgot about Osage and Manchester
Our apartment across from the Forum?!
I got Lakers in my bones
I forgot Inglewood,
Centinela Church

Pastor John and Jan Jones
The Fox Hills hospital, I forgot my sister had
  epilepsy
I forgot to thank the faith of Dr. Holden who
  knew she would outgrow it
I forgot my mom was adventurous and saw a
  world outside of L.A.
had not been for it I'd a been crippin with the
  twins
Dwayne and Dwight,
I didn't know of Ethiopia, that you were showing
  in my cheekbone, or the Bantu and Togo region
  screaming you one of us.
Thank you to the Golden Ox on Florence and
  Main,
I forgot that alleyway behind it almost stole my
  innocence.
I was only 10.
Thank you Azusa
The burritos at La Tolteca
Thank you Uptown Whittier
DJ Bobbito
Larry Acosta
UYWI, 08
Legacy, Kareem, Brian Dye they the way I met
  Lecrae.
Me and T.J. politic'd for hours with 116 Clique at
  that Chipotle

I would not be the same if Crae aint take me on
    Unashamed
TDOT A.T. BJ Andy Mineo had us grooving at
    his wedding
Amisho Baraka
We deeply miss DJ official
And still aint removed him from our group text to
    this day.
Thank you Catalyst
Q conference
Bob Goff
Tyler Regan.
Brad Lomenick,
Zane Black,
Montana crew.
Condap
The Refuge.
Jonathan Block and Merritt
This book is a consequence of y'alls vote of
    confidence
Science Mike, Lisa, David, Michael Gungor,
Terence Clark,
John Ardt
Audrey Assad
Will and Dre.
The blessings of Austin, Sarah, Katlin, and
    Rachel Held Evans
Jeff Chu

Hatmakers, I'm so sorry Hatmakers.
Judah Smith, Tori Kelly and André
Kjlh DJ MAAAAAAALSKI
Yo Pastor Zakiya Jackson,
My dawg Derek Minor, who picked me up when
thought my career was done
My designated shooter, Pray for JGivens
Oside Johnny
Jabee, Murs, Micah B,
Shorty Doowop learning her worth is more than
her body.
Shout out Long Beach for handing me my baby
Soul!
Jay King, Gabby, Mikaela, Andrew, Shawsome
If you seen me you seen them
All the Table turners
DJ Sean P
EL hefe, in west LA, my 1st Road dawgs DJ
Promote and Valerie.
If you seen me you seen him
He's throwing hands up in heaven
No words to express how much I miss him
The Killapino, The b-boy pinoy, Mr.
Humblebeastro.
E for EFECHTOOOOOOO!
Finally the closest to me Alma Luna Soul
Thank you 2020 quarantine for showing me just
how much I need my family.

THE TRUTH IS YELLING AT YOU

"THERE IS A METAPHOR IN THERE SOMEWHERE"

He looked peculiarly,
as is his practice, at the site he's seen many times
in many places
His only thought . . .
"There is a metaphor in there somewhere"

NOTICING THE TRUTH
HIDING IN PLAIN SIGHT

Let me tell you about the second-whitest email I've ever gotten. (If you're lucky, one day I'll tell you about THE whitest email I've ever gotten.) It came from what turned out to be a phenomenal organization called Great Objects (a part of the Gates Foundation) that does remarkable justice work across the globe. Little did I know at that time that the "Gates" in the Gates Foundation was Bill Gates. He wanted to meet me once but I didn't connect the dots until much later. Stupid Prop. I digress. Back to this extremely, utterly white email.

Now some of you might be asking, "What in the world is a 'white email'?!" That is a fair question. After all, emails are not persons, therefore they can't claim any socioethnic ties. It's ridiculous to call objects a race. Race, of course, is a social construct anyway. However, objects can have characteristics consistent with characteristics of a group of people. For example, I shop at Black stores all the time. What makes the store Black? The items that are sold there like Blue Magic, Royal Crown, TCB, and flat irons. Don't know what I'm talking about? I'm not even gonna tell you. Just know these things are vital for the survival of Black people, we know exactly what to do with these products. Confused? That's the way I felt about this email!

The email was inviting me on an all-expenses-paid camping trip in a forest located a couple hours outside of Nashville, Tennessee. Now, stop right here . . . You tell me how wise it is to follow white people into the forest outside of Nashville, Tennessee?! After reading the email, I said to myself, *Let me get this straight.* (Actually, before I try to get this straight, can we just talk about how white people love camping? To be honest, I kind of don't get it! Civilization has moved forward, we figured out that it's better to be inside than outside. Why in the world would I make myself, by choice, go outside?!) Now, back to getting this straight. I was thinking, *You're going to spend all this money to bring me and nineteen other "influencers" to this forest where we'll talk about feeding people rather than actually feeding people?! WYPIPO!*

Even though I wasn't sure about the whole thing, I decided to go. Moral of the story is, try new things! Turns out camping was one of the most fun things I've ever done. I got to use my AeroPress to make coffee—stay with me—outside! I saw some of the most beautiful land I've ever seen. I now totally get all these camping Instagram accounts you all follow. It's beautiful. The soil is truly sacred.

Perhaps the most important part of that trip for me was something I learned about perspective. While we were there, the organizers showed us a video (turns out this camping was *glamping* so we actually slept very comfortably indoors) of some astronauts, and they talked about something called the overview effect (check out *The Overview Effect* by Frank White if you want to get nerdy and learn more).

The overview effect is the idea that everyone who has seen the earth from space reports the same effect: awe. When astronauts look at our planet from space, they are in absolute awe at how beautiful the earth is, blown away by seeing hurricanes from above, by watching day turn to night and then the darkness lighting up as cities come to life.

Something else that becomes more clear from the vantage point of space is that, of course, the names of the states are not written across the land. Unlike our maps, the word *California* isn't written on the top of California, and it doesn't say across the span of Africa A-F-R-I-C-A. Why? Because borders are something that humans created. Seeing it from space, you get the sense that the globe is just one thing. It's one living object. And we are literally in this together. Like it or not, we are all we got. At least until we actually connect with the aliens. But if they are as smart as we picture them, they are probably actively hiding from all our cameras. (I picture them moving behind the Mars rover's camera making sure it's never pointing directly at them.) So until we connect, we are all we got. When seen from that perspective, our problems become smaller, and the things we fight over are, actually, pretty stupid because we are all we got! There is only one soil, and we all sprang from it. What a metaphor. The overview effect.

In this chapter, we're talking about truth. And what I've learned about truth is that it is all around us; our job is to pay attention and listen. The truth is yelling at you! Dude, the planet itself is sayin:

Psst, xenophobia is stupid. Your borders are made up.

Psst, the planet is alive. The rocks, the water, the vegetation, and the creatures that live on the rocks, in the water, and consume the vegetation—it's all alive.

Psst, you're all neighbors.

PSST, perspective changes things. Maybe your vantage point is limited. Maybe someone from outside your world can give you a little perspective about the inside of your world. Maybe hollering at some people from other nations or other socioeconomic statuses could give you a good perspective on your own, as well as empathy for the other.

This is what I mean by "true."

If we slow down for a second, really be present in a moment, even in the most mundane of moments, if we allow ourselves to examine our memories with this one question in mind, "What's this moment telling me about me, about the world?," we might discover a new and better way to relate to ourselves and others. This is much less about the high philosophical work of exploring the nature of truth, but rather, as we do the work of terraforming, this is the stage where we survey what's already available, look for what we might have missed, and learn what those things can do to make our lives and the planet better. And it starts with hearing and then listening.

HOW TO HEAR

If the truth is all around us, and we just need to listen, then how come we seem to miss it? I say the truth is yelling, but sometimes we just don't hear it, or maybe we heard wrong. Let me give you an example.

When I was growing up, my aunt NeNe lived on 87th and Broadway, in a small two-bedroom apartment with my uncle Sonny. My sister and I were the only nieces and nephews that were allowed to spend the night at their house. "They the only ones raised right!" Uncle Sonny would say.

On those occasions, I spent most of the day playing with the Hot Wheels and action figures my aunt kept for me in the spare room. Then I'd go outside and play with the boys on the block. I rode in the back of that EL Dawg, up Manchester to Crenshaw for groceries with Auntie and my sister. They were great days.

At night, Uncle Sonny's '81 Cadillac Eldorado would come roaring into the carport around 10:30 or 11:00 p.m. after his hard day's work at LAX. When we were spending the weekend with them, my sister and I would be doing our best to stay up to see him. I would rarely make it. We would be sprawled out on blankets on the brown carpet in front of their huge tube television, you know, the ones that look like pieces of furniture complete with the wood carvings along the side. That thing would take at least four minutes to warm up after we turned it on.

Uncle Sonny was the absolute archetype of a 1970s LA man. Forged in all that is South Central, an Eastsider, two brothers, two sisters, all of them active gang members except him. He was a hard-working, Afro-rocking, one-woman man. Tuff as nails and gentle as a dove. He would plop down on the couch and I would watch his ritual through the haze of my dozing. He opened a shoe box, flipped the top upside down, placed it on his lap, and would lay out a small bag of green.

"What's that, Uncle?"

"Them my cigarettes. Did you have fun today?"

(Narrator: they aren't cigarettes.)

About five years later, Aunt NeNe and Uncle Sonny would have a son, my baby cousin Brandon (who ain't a baby at all now). My uncle succumbed to cancer shortly after. After college, I was reminiscing with my sister about those days trying to stay up to play with Uncle Sonny, bummed that my cousin Brandon doesn't really have much of a memory of his dad. I mentioned how loved I felt by Auntie for having those toys just for me. She wouldn't ever let me take them home, which I thought was strange but I trusted her.

"What toys?" my sister asked.

"Those lil Hot Wheels that were in the spare room!"

"Oh, those were Derek's toys."

"WHO?!"

"Derek. It was his room and his toys."

"WHO IN THE HELL IS DEREK?!" I yelled.

"What?!" asked my sister, looking at me like I was crazy. "He's Uncle Sonny's son."

"HUH?!"

"You know, Uncle Sonny had a son before he married NeNe."

"WHAT ARE YOU TALKING ABOUT?!"

"You don't remember DEREK?"

"NAW! WHAT THE HELL?!"

Learning about Derek made me realize that as a child, I had one understanding of what was true, which was that my aunt and uncle didn't have any children but kept toys for me to play with in a spare room. As an adult that history got majorly revised—turns out what I didn't know was apparently I have a cousin named Derek who lived with his birth mother and visited his father (my uncle Sonny) on the weekends that I wasn't present. Mind blown.

Have you ever heard of history revisionism? According to the expert that is Wikipedia, it's defined as:

> The re-interpretation of an historical
> account. It usually involves challenging
> the orthodox (established, accepted or
> traditional) views held by professional scholars
> about an historical event or time-span or
> phenomenon, introducing contrary evidence,
> or reinterpreting the motivations and decisions
> of the people involved. The revision of the
> historical record can reflect new discoveries of
> fact, evidence, and interpretation, which then
> results in revised history. In dramatic cases,
> revisionism involves a reversal of older moral
> judgments.[1]

We revise history all the time. Maps that were drawn pre–Christopher Columbus's voyages are missing three entire continents. Europe had no idea the Americas or Antarctica existed! They were there the whole time, it's not like the Western Hemisphere just materialized when Leif Erikson touched down. Entire civilizations came and went on this land. After the discoveries of the "new world" (which, in fact, isn't new at all, it's the same age as the rest of the world, it was just new to Europeans), Europe had to redraw all its maps and rewrite its world history.

In the wing of Christianity I came up in, we were taught that revising our understanding of what the Bible says is dangerous, because it undermines inerrancy (which is a fancy word that means the Bible is without any errors). However, inerrancy assumes the authors who wrote the various parts of the Bible had an omniscient perspective, even though the Bible was written by human authors, who wrote based on the way they saw the world. When we view the biblical writers as exceptional, *that* actually undermines the beauty and relevance of the Bible. No! The magic is the fact that the Bible is profoundly human. God reveals himself to humans, no matter where they are in their understanding. The people in our bibles thought the stars were located in heaven, we think they are burning balls of gas millions of miles away. Who knows, we might learn something different in a hundred years.

My homie Pete Enns, in his book *How the Bible Actually Works*, gives an example of this by examining the Book of Proverbs. That book was written for a ruling class, for people preparing to take over a nation. That ain't us. But by the time we get to the era the gospels take place in, Proverbs has already been retooled to be understood as a book of wisdom for all Jews; then by Acts, for Jew and gentile. History revised.

Finding out Derek existed revised history for me. That revision, that new information, tuned my ears to a truth that had been there all along, I just hadn't heard it. There was one story of beauty and truth that was saying to me, "Wow! My auntie cared enough about me, a boy who is not even her son, to make sure I had playthings. She treated me as her own." I heard that loud and clear. But there was a whole other layer of truth that was yelling that I couldn't hear at all. The full story shows that my aunt has the capacity to love beyond what I could possibly imagine. She has a heart big enough to carry two boys who are not her sons. And this is a truth I had no idea I would need as an adult. I grew up to marry a single parent myself. I, too, learned to love a kid who was not my own as if she were. I had no idea this gem was just sitting in my past. It wasn't that

I wasn't listening to the yelling truth; I just didn't hear it.

What is there in your story that might be worth going back and revisiting? Like I found, there might be some beauty and joy collecting dust in your past. It might be buried under some pain, and maybe it would be helpful to walk through with a mental health professional who is trained in helping you make sense of it. We touched on this idea in the "Tell Better Origin Stories" chapter. Revising ain't bad; that new information could help you hear some truth you didn't even know you missed. And maybe that could even bring some healing.

Or maybe the opposite is true. Maybe you are remembering something with rose-colored glasses, romanticizing a time long gone, one that actually sucked if you let yourself slow down and really listen. Here's the thing: even if it's painful, don't look away. Polish up those moments. Gather new perspectives, ask other people who might have been around. There is some beauty even in the pain. It was there the whole time.

ONCE YOU HEAR, YOU BETTER LISTEN

Not hearing is very different from not listening. When we don't hear the yelling truth, that can be due to any number of totally understandable reasons. In the story about my cousin Derek, I honestly just didn't know, I was never told the full story until much later. It's a whole other story when you do know, when you hear something loud and clear and decide to not listen to it. Let me tell you about a time I went from hearing to listening.

A couple years ago I just walked in the door after a three-day trip. It was a short trip home, since I had to catch a red-eye flight that night. Alma and our eldest daughter, Luna, were having what seemed to be a real heart-to-heart. My daughter is off to the races with preteen middle-school drama, girl tribes, Snapchat crush confessions, and grape-flavored vape pens. Luna had been a bit "mouthy" (mouthy—that's so Black) before I left, so I had my thoughts about what was going on. Alma had clearly just finished a good cry. Anyone's natural response would be, "What's wrong?" That was my response too!

"NOTHING!" Luna says.

"Clearly nothing is not what happened, y'all," I reply.

"Yeah, I just don't want to tell you."

"Well, guess I'll just go back to Florida then."

(I know that last line is petty but that is my last name so there is that.)

I'm a card-carrying member of the small fraternity of dads of only daughters. Membership requirements are of course the obvious—only having daughters—and also feeling like the whole house speaks a language you don't. Everyone in the house easily understands one another, while Dad is basically a refugee who is responsible for cleaning hair out of various drains and who continually inserts himself into interactions that the nonverbals say he's really not welcomed to, but lowkey, to not try is to fail. Tis quite a conundrum that I wouldn't trade for the world.

As a parent who travels a lot for work, the reality is the house has to move on and function when I'm not here. Alma and our girls have to set up systems that work for them. I understand that, and yet still, upon my arrival back home, it sinks in again that life didn't stop and wait for my triumphant reentry. The kids have not planned a ticker tape parade. Instead, my return can be very disruptive and invasive to the rhythm they've gotten in.

For the rest of that evening, I fumbled pretty much every interaction. I held my tongue and listened to inside jokes between my wife and kids. I saw the good practices I tried to set up with my kids, like make your bed when you get up, be completely dismissed. Or at least, that's how it felt.

I was probably just really tired. Well, there is no "probably" about it. I was tired and I just missed them. I probably drank too much the night before. Could have been a million things. All I know is I felt like I didn't matter in the one place I absolutely need to matter.

(I know what you're thinking. *Oh poor you, Prop! In your Long Beach house next to the shore, coming home from adoring fans!* You're right, I have it good, but I need you to feel what I was feeling at the moment. We all have moments that our behaviors don't match our character.)

I essentially shut down for the rest of the evening. When I tried to bathe my two-year-old, she just shouted: "NOT YOU DADDY! MOMMY ONLY!" The whole time. Okay, full disclosure, I didn't mind not having to do the bath, but still, rejection sucks. As I'm trying to bathe her, I'm listening to Alma and Luna giggle, trade stories, and just be best buds.

The girls went off to bed. Alma noticed my mood and gave me the look. The look that says, *I see that you goin through a thing and I know you haven't asked for help but you know you need it and I won't say anything but just know that I know.* Yes, that look. When you are truly known by another person, your body will tell a truth your mouth refuses to verify.

———

Your eyes just won't keep they mouth shut.

———

At 9:30 p.m., I kissed Alma good-bye and headed on over to pick up DJ Efechto en route to the airport. It's funny how moods work. Feeling down about one area of life infects other areas that ain't have anything to do with the other! My evening spent feeling unwanted at home now had me noticing how much wasn't going right professionally. Could be my three wing two talking, but who knows. Around this time, Humble Beastro, Efechto's cooking and catering service, was really taking off, so I was losing my DJ, too. My internal monologue was racing:

> Dang, Prop! You ain't won no Grammy. Not even a Dove award for crying out loud.
> Why haven't you done late-night TV?
> Where is your NPR Tiny Desk session?
> You are the king of "almost," ain't you, Prop?!
> And to top it all off, your kids don't want you!

At the airport, DJ Efechto and I breezed through the frequent traveler routine: stroll through precheck, early boarding, window seat, left side of the plane, hoodie and earplugs. NIGHT NIGHT!

But this night the routine was off. We got the wack seat! And no upgrade so no stupid little drink before flight. I know, poor me, right?! I promise you I'm about to learn a great lesson so don't write me off yet.

Truth is fresh dressed
Like a million bucks,
Waving her hands,
Yelling at the top of her lungs,
Standing on its head,
You pissed at the Wi-Fi
It's too slow.

We finally settled in and I'm ready to knock out. I'm still in a bad mood, feeling kinda depressed, but since it's a red-eye, I'm going to have to be ready to entertain when we land, so sleep is crucial. Then comes the announcement:

"Ladies and gentlemen, from the flight deck this is First Officer Gonzalez. It seems we can't locate our pilot and captain. We are waiting to hear from him and as soon as we do we will let you know."

No big deal, I've been through every possible

flight delay. Once on the way to SXSW, the connection flight between Dallas and Austin got delayed because, get this, the oven that heats the meals for purchase wasn't working. Really? A forty-five-minute flight? No one ever buys the food. Are y'all serious? I continued to doze off.

One.

Hour.

Later.

"Ladies and gentlemen we have no idea what happened to our pilot. Next pilot won't be available until 6:30 a.m. so we're gonna go ahead and deplane. Agents will be out there to assist in rebooking. Thank you for your patience."

I always hate that last line. Thank you for my patience?! You act like we had a choice. I don't know what it is about deplaning but it's the most demoralizing part of flight delays. Something about it seems so final. Either way, all I'm thinking is how this is the exact way this night was expected to go because life sucks and I'm a failed artist and unwanted father.

The rescheduled flight wasn't until the next morning, so Efechto suggested we go back to his house to sleep for a few hours. I remember feeling so depressed, like life sucked and nothing could make it better. Somehow, that short ride back to Tita Helen's house (DJ Efechto's momma is Tita Helen) really snapped me back into reality. I realized I was being yelled at by beauty and truth, but I was only hearing pain and abandonment.

Beauty was saying, "Listen, Prop, you ain't depressed, you are mildly inconvenienced! There are people out here really dealing with depression. You just forgot. You forgot the forces all around you that make the life you lead possible. You forgot you get paid to rap and talk about stuff you talk about on your own couch. You forgot your wife is light-years smarter than you and still procreated with your dumb ass. You forgot God is present. You forgot the grace that you never needed to notice. You forgot, you live in exile waiting for Eden to be made right again."

Just like the astronauts experienced a perspective shift from space, I experienced a perspective shift in that car. That moment forced me to slow down and realize I hadn't been listening to the truth that was yelling at me, telling me that I was valuable, that I had a good life, that beauty was all around me.

I guess it came down to slowing down enough to notice that truth. Imagine building a world, a way of life, that is always on the hunt for the unnoticed, that spots the beauty as easily as we spot flaws. That hunts for the amazing in each other. That rehearses that skill, and has an involuntary habit of pointing at the beauty of the normal. What if our feeds were full of the beauty of the normal? It's crazy how much has to go right for our lives to function normally—not even extraordinarily amazing, just normal. I have no idea what happened to the pilot that day. I take at least twelve flights a month. In all those flights, the pilots didn't get stuck in traffic, didn't have fights with their spouses, weren't too sleepy to fly, flight attendants didn't get stuck at TSA, and no one in air traffic control had car trouble. If you think about it, it's quite a symphony of happenstances, playing a concert right in front of us. And still, truth is yelling at you all the time. By not slowing down to listen, it led to me telling myself a bad story. I've learned I gotta slow down and listen to the beauty of the normal. It's probably the hardest thing for me to get this truth into my soul. But it sure does make for good poetry.

IF COFFEE WERE A MAN

If coffee were a man, it'd be a Black man,
Joyous
Welcoming
Warm.

Life giving.
He ain't for everyone
An acquired taste
Bold adaptable.
He'd give himself for your good.
Share the fruits of his grind and sweat.
Neither heat nor pressure would scare him.
He would and does flourish come hell and
    hot water
He'd welcome both for he knows
It brings out what's best in him.
He would not mind the crushing and the grind,
    his is more or less a Porlex.
His creative process is a natural
Sun washed
His is single origin in nature namely north
    African
Yet could flourish in multiple regions when the
    climate is suitable
South Central American,
Afro Latin.
Micronesian
He'd find joy workin with the indigenous. He'd
    enjoy their blends and what flavor their music
    notes might bring.
If coffee were a man
He be a Black man
He would be shipped by force

His course would be grind and grind he must.
If coffee were a man, he'd be exhausted
Yet required to wake all up.
He'd be looked to as cure for the morning blues yet
    no one would consider his.
His second impression would feel more like
    appropriation not appreciation.
He'd feel like he been working in fields making
    gourmet from scraps,
from the overlooked
only to get his meal handed to the very hands that
    passed him over.
If coffee were a woman, she'd be a Black woman.
Strong beautiful,
Delicate
Elegant
well-traveled
complex.
Actually exponentially more complex than fine
    wine.
Remember when she went abroad
Vienna
Turkey
Spain
Collaboration was amazing.
She would have explored the world
she would be naturally washed, exotic
With a cultured palate.

Elevation would not scare her, she would thrive in
regions others can't.
They can't breathe the air up there.
If coffee were a person,
haunting sense of irony would be inescapable
What was once a centuries-old practice of
populous has become a global craze made only
for pompous.
How?
The irony of how something so black is so white
She would get heated up and watered down and
mixed with white cream and artificial sweetener
for those who couldn't stomach her purity.
For them
She would be too strong
And bitter.
And simultaneously
Then the purist would say they liked the black in
you, only.
If coffee were a mother,
She would lead well.
Would say there's a way we could make art together,
beautiful lattes
Swirling flowers.
Lovely swans.
Where black white and brown dance and make
blossoms
and we could cold brew up experiments with
mocha, nitrogen

Where bitter and sweet harmonize their beautiful
   notes.
If coffee were a person,
They'd beg to not profit off our backs and use our
   farmers' faces for marketing to those who don't
   want us in their country in the first place
If coffee were a man
Coffee would say there's a fourth way.
That black brown and white can dance again.
As curious and magical as morning dew and
   espresso. We could go in and uplift each other.
They would say we have gifts and so do you. Let
   us not be elitist. We are
Coffee by the people for the people
Fourth wave coffee is coffee for the people.

TWO MINUTES THIRTY SECONDS

For two minutes and thirty seconds
We were on Pangea
we were one country.
Me and my grandad were the same age.
Two minutes and thirty seconds we saw how small
   we were.
We saw how privileged we were to be able to see
   how small we are.
We saw Black was beautiful
And mixed metaphors can still speak volumes.

how not only Black was beautiful but when
   shadows block out the light the light shows
   its brilliance it didn't even know it had! We
   should trust Black more.
The planet knew we needed it.
We were two days from Nazis marching on
   American soil spitting irony on our legacy
our "greatest generation" Rhetoric
We were two days away from a car driving into
   Peace.
White lives matter
Blood and soil
Appropriated Polynesian
Mosquito repellent turned white hoods
Tiki torch turned burning crosses
We used to be one planet
2:30 our perspective was orbital
Wouldn't you know it, the words "United States"
   isn't written on the ground when you look at
   Earth from space!
Streaked across globe
Streamed revolution televised
Bend Oregon highways turned one ways to handle
   the traffic
Kim Jong Un sang Bob Marley
Vlad French kisses Trump and
Tinashe squashed beef with Cornel
Biggie and Tupac did Music together.
Elvis finally admitted to biting

Weinstein thought twice about unzipping
Stormy Daniels and the prophet Daniel
Drank thunderbird.
And Meek was free.
2:30 seconds. I straightened out my side eye at
   Red caps.
Hippies and hula-hoops
Who cared about traffic on the 405.
Heavenly bodies showed off curves
And glorious stretch marks.
Space is sexy.
We let our appetite for destruction satiate for a sec
Was you too cool for the glasses?
Was you too stupid to not look directly at it?
Did our president actually look directly at it after
   EVERY SCIENTIST said not to?
Did you laugh?
You ever make out wit someone you know you
   shouldn't?
You ever touched something that said don't touch?
You ever seen an eclipse?
The Milky Way?
You been to Stonehenge?
You ever felt connected to Mayans and Druids at
   the same time?
Dogons, Etruscans, Moors, and Ethiopians.
Have you ever experienced something that was
   so far above you, and was going to happen
   whether you were there or not? Yet it felt like

the entirety of the cosmos conspired just to show
you something about yourself?
2:30
Can't wait for the next one.

TWENTY YEARS

Twenty years.
But who's counting right?
Twenty years of a said marriage where she
  ain't necessarily have a say in its original
  arrangement nor the terms thereof
But twenty years.
A man beats his wife for twenty years,
Somehow she musters up the quote unquote
  bravery to stay, though, because one day he
  decided maybe he shouldn't hit her no more.
  Now granted that was due to outside pressure
  which threatened the size of his pockets but he
  stopped nonetheless
But the damage is done.
And on their fortieth anniversary they throw a
  huge shindig
Invite all their friends, they spare no expenses.
She expected to smile. Celebrate her husband's
  greatness

*How far they have come as a country, WAIT, I
mean a couple.*

*We are to reminisce and run slideshows of all the
great Trumps I MEAN
Triumphs.
Of all the wonderful lands and homes they stole
WAIT I mean
Conquered, I'M SORRY, visited.
And in silence before any guests arrived you can
hear the creak of the wooden floors as he walks
over to her and ever-so gently rubs the small of
her back before the show starts and says
"Baby look how far I've come no need to mention
the first twenty years because talking about
it will make everyone uncomfortable and it
separates why would you want to separate?
"Why would you bring up old stuff?"
What is she supposed to do?
Simple.
She is to stand smiling holding her sparklers
Wearing her pretty little red white and blue
dress and act like the first twenty years didn't
happen.
Act like she still ain't suffering under the thumb of
his mental walls built?
He ain't hit no more. But he don't have to. The
scars do all that for him.*

The police, I MEAN, the support group helps
  keep them in line.
She really aint been the same.
Her hip kinda out of place so back curves kinda
  weird,
Her jaw a slightly ajar to left so she smile a lil
  crooked
Yet she's compared to the other wives when she
  ain't around
She ain't as pretty as the rest of em but says to
  her he don't really see color, I MEAN beauty.
She is to enjoy her newly found rights, I MEAN
  her big house she can actually live in now.
Her rights to vote, you know, on what's for
  dinner.
She kinda got it good now
Her life is good. Well at least better.
She should pat your nation, I MEAN her man
  on his back. Tell him he's the greatest coun . . .
  excuse me, man, in the world
Some might ask why she didn't leave?
Why she make it all about her,
Don't other wives get hit too?
Don't all wives matter?
Why is her suffering more important?
Why we gotta mourn her bruises
When girls hit girls all the time?
I think it's called wife on wife crime.

And furthermore IF it was so bad
Why was he not prosecuted?
You ask why would all their friends gather around
and allow this to happen?
Why does her church silence her and call her
problems a social issue?
Maybe she's making this up!
And in a magical plot twist she is now the villain
if she talks about this?
He owes her! Right? Right.
Does not forgiveness require restitution?
Does not the cross you say you cling to mean
Reconciliation comes after justice?
What about the ladies who punched back?
But we all know Vengeance is a bastard form of
Justice.
But can you at least sympathize?
So why has he not given her back her twenty
years or at least try to?
Is it too late to say sorry?
Huh, Justice?
But ya know what, never mind it's none of my
business
Happy Fourth of July everyone.
Enjoy your ribs.

IT WAS THERE ALL ALONG

There is something that makes you the best at
    what you do.
Different than all others. And I'm not gonna lie.
    It's kinda weird.
You are artists, but not like the rest of us.
You see both painting and canvas. And affirm
    they are both art in their own right.
You are backdrop and principle and can
    interchange them effortlessly.
Stone and sculpture and can't tell which is more
    beautiful.
You don't see two individuals. You see the
    marriage, literally.
What the hell?
Only poetry can explain your eyes.
You have an extra set of pupils.
You see past and future.
You walk into a room and don't see what we see.
No wait, not only do you see what you see you
    actually see what we see and can't see but make
    us see it.
It's weird.
You see possibility.
You create imagination while painting with
    someone else's.
I was told when I started doing poetry,

Don't tell us,
take us there.
You have five paintbrushes.
Use them all or don't use them at all.
A true poet doesn't just tell us how she feels,
She tells us how WE FEEL.
As if Words and images reach into the small
*   of the crowds, back and the poem is animating*
*   my mouth and squeezing truth out of my*
*   lungs.*
You take our breath away
You transform sketchbook into nostalgia
Storyboard to true story.
You are the best at this
How you read mind and heart.
You are at your worst servant leaders and at your
*   best Mozart.*
Pieces of perfect symmetry.
Mozarts of irony.
Vincent van Gogh who only paints with
*   serendipity.*
Dippin your brushes in to messy blotches of
*   coincidences*
And attacks a living canvas like every splatter has
*   a destiny.*
Where would we be without you?
What is story with no setting?
Plot with no context

You see context.
Better than any of us.
Better than all of us.
There is something that makes you different,
   special.
Better.
It's this.
You make us better.

TERRAFORMING
PROJECT 3

I. PAY ATTENTION TO YOUR RITUALS.
I imagine you have a number of rituals in
your life. Many times our rituals become
mindless and automatic, and it's possible
that if you slowed down and noticed, they
might be yelling some truth to you. Let's
get meta! Write down a list of rituals that
might actually be telling you something
about yourself. Something that demands
examining.

For me, one example is my love for
coffee. I started to wonder why I got so
obsessed with doing a task that takes me
ten to fifteen minutes when in actuality, it
could take two minutes?! Is it taste? That's

part of it. But mostly, it's the love of art and the need to slow down. I was a drawing and painting major in college. I realized I love the *art* of coffee, how long it takes and how much variation is possible in one cup. It's the same thing that drew me to making cocktails, the art of the process. Not only do I enjoy it, it also makes me slow down. I lead a superbusy life, so the moments where I'm making a cup of coffee or a cocktail are the slowest, most focused moments of my day. Now it's your turn. What is that thing you do or think that is trying to tell you something? Bring that lesson into your new world. Terraform your brain!

2. NOTICE BEAUTY IN THE NORMAL. Think about your normal day, what has to go right for your day to work? Notice the things you never noticed—like the streetlights working, the gas station having gas, the strong wood beams that hold up your house. Try to go through one workday where you focus on noticing the everyday wonders that have to go right and have been going right for years.

3. LISTEN TO YOUR LIFE. How often do we slow down and really ask ourselves why

we do or think the way we do? I started to
do this and it led to all the poetry in this
chapter. Here's an example. Start by reading
the "I Hate Cats" poem below.

I HATE CATS

See, when I would leave for tour, my wife and
  my daughter—
(Well, this was before my baby daughter
  was born)
They would—they would bond by going to these
  animal shelters
And playing with the cats and see, here's the
  thing:
I hate cats
Well, hate is a strong word
It's just that I'm a dog person
And cats—demon spawn, see I don't trust 'em
They always looking like they planning a murder,
  right?
Like cats be putting in work
You ever watched a movie?
What does the weird old lady have?
What about the villain's pet? They evil!
See, ancient Egyptians, they knew that and they
  built the pyramids
So they was onto something, right?

Well, I would receive these—these terrifying
*   pictures in my texts*
Of my daughter smiling in the throes of full bliss
Holding what has to be the biggest letdown of a
*   cousin*
I mean, cats are related to lions
You share taxonomy with tigers—tigers!
Why are you so cupcake?
Why does my daughter wanna bring you home?
Of all things, a cat!
See, I hate cats!
Well, hate is a strong word, you know what I'm
*   saying?*
Don't get me wrong, I'm not like a—like a bigot
*   or nothing*
I mean, it's not like I like . . . I mean, I don't see
*   species, you know what I mean?*
My babysitter, when I was a kid, see, she had
*   a cat*
And I'm sure there are nice God-fearing people
*   that have cats in they house*
It's just not in my home, see, they stink
They be rubbin' they terrible pheromones all over
*   my furniture*
But alas, kicking and screaming, I forced a smile
*   on my face when my daughter brings this*
*   terrible thing home*
I'm gonna be honest: I thought I raised her better
*   than that!*

See, we are a dog family, we stick to our own kind
Why couldn't you love a dog?
This is just the voice of a concerned father, see
See, people may think a certain way about her
when she walk down the street
And why you walking a cat anyway?
They gon' think I ain't raised my child well
And it's not like this cat has done anything to me
personally
I just know they kind, I mean, I seen 'em on
the news
They be tearing up the homes they owners provide
for 'em
Why would you tear up your own home?
How come cats can't be grateful?
Why are all cats lazy?
They be complainin' about they oppression
You see it in they eyes
Don't the people that take care of you take care of
you well?
Haven't we had cats in the White House?
Ain't that enough?
But then this cat got in my house and, to be
honest, it was kind of different
I actually enjoyed my time with him,
but—but—but—
But the—but the point is I love my daughter
And I've already made my decision
And it's not the cat's fault

I just hate they kind
Well . . . hate is a strong word
It's just my heritage, I come from a dog family
It's heritage, not hate, right?
Hate's a strong word
We still talkin' about cats, right?

The poem is just as much about racism (if you didn't figure that out already, yes, it's about racism) as it is deeply personal. It's me, asking myself, *What is my reason for holding on to this habitual hatred toward a whole species?* Especially when I've never owned a cat until my daughter brought one home, and then I actually fell in love with it! When I really listened, truth said, "Looks like the problem is you, Prop." I realized I'm holding on to an imaginary version of myself that is seeking to maintain some sort of machismo reputation in the eyes of other men, who also only exist in my imagination. I wonder how many other areas in my life I do this to myself?

What is an area of your life that you could reexamine? Ask yourself why you think this way about a certain person, or group of people, or a policy, or a program, or anything, and then write it down. You could even turn this into a poem!

THE
SOIL

SOIL IS SACRED

THAT MUD IS MAGIC

Snow flurries and pine trees,
Flowers and butterflies
All watch with bated breath
For the day the human figures it out
None of us are on Earth,
we are Earth.

ALL THE LAND
IS SACRED LAND

The first national tour I ever went on as a solo artist was with a Native American artist named RedCloud. He took me to twenty-seven reservations. Along the way, the people who lived on these reservations taught me things that have shaped not only the way I see the world but also the way I see God.

On the Cherokee rez in Oklahoma, over dinner, one of the tribesmen was schooling me. "You know, in our culture, human beings can't own soil because we didn't make it. How can you own something you didn't make?" When European settlers tried to buy land from them, they thought that was the strangest question. I often picture that interaction. Just a comedy of miscommunication. "Uhhh . . . you wanna buy that rock too?" All hilarious until the deaths start happening, of course. So, if we didn't make the ground but we all have access to the ground, then the ground is a gift given to us by our Creator. Like it or not, we are sharing it. And the ground, since it is a gift from God, is sacred. And they had this phrase called the "earth man," which is the idea that you and I are made from the ground, the soil. And if the soil is sacred and a gift from our Creator, and you are made of the soil, then you are a gift and sacred too.

It's interesting to think about how these ancient tribes beat our ninth-grade biology classes to the punch. Because eventually we all learn that we are in fact made of the soil—the elements in Earth are the same elements that make our bodies. Let me push you a little harder. You don't get past the first page of your bible before God tells you the same thing. You are made of the soil. And at the end of the day, whether it's red soil, black soil, or white soil, it's the same earth. And it's all a gift.

BROWN EARTH PHOENIX

You are what you are
How dare you
Let death sing a song that could scare you
You are what you are
I swear if you ever think less of yourself
Let me declare
She would take the wings of the morning and fly
*   to the uttermost parts of the sea*
Find She in the Galapagos.
But you are what you are, sis, a brown skin
*   Phoenix*
My request is when you look at you, remind you
*   you need this*

I'm here to submit to you,
No literally submit to you humbly come under you
You are Falcon a bird of prey
Doubting is beneath you
How could you let these silly boys
Question your genius
Where are you going?
You are what you are
We are seed you sown
You are born of the air, look down at hurricane
The wisdom you share proves we ain't insane
Sing ya song bird
Do ya dance girl
Ya advance girl
This your world
You are what you are
Let the truth haunt you
Only you can stop you

YOU HAVE ALWAYS BEEN
ONE WITH THE LAND

You ever heard of the "Earth Sandwich?" It's a silly story meant to make the point that humans are connected to the earth. I first heard it told by my ace, Michael Gungor. We were preparing for the last Gungor tour, and it was me, The Brilliance, and Science Mike sitting in the Liturgists studio in Highland Park. Highland Park is pretty much the Williamsburg of Los Angeles, the most gentrified part of town. When I was growing up, if you needed to hire a coyote, or get your grandma in El Salvador a fake social security card, you had to go talk to the Veteranos in the Avenues. The sets in Highland Park are called the Avenues because the street names are all formatted the same, the word *Avenue* and a number. Ave 51, Ave 52, and so on. Those fake papers would cost you about 2k and most likely you're still going to get robbed on the way out. Better speak a little Spanish or know someone in that hood. Now, the Gungors live there and Alma's sunrise hot yoga class is held there every Tuesday. Gentrify, baby, gentrify!

Michael Gungor starts in on this story that ends in hysterical laughter from everyone else and complete confusion from me.

"I saw an experiment where two friends wanted to make an earth sandwich. So they got two slices of bread. Placed one on the ground. Then calculated the literal direct opposite place on the other side of the world and flew there, then placed the other slice of bread on the ground. As in, if you could draw a straight line through the earth from one slice to another, the line would be perfectly straight. The earth made itself a sandwich! GET IT?! THE EARTH MADE ITSELF A SANDWICH!"

At this point Lisa Gungor, Michael's wife, is in tears laughing. I am channeling all the facial expressions Black people have when we see white people play quidditch. I'm clearly missing something. "So they actually spent money and time to fly to the other side of the earth to place a piece of bread on the ground?"

"Yes! It's an earth sandwich, the earth made itself a sandwich!" says Michael between his laughs.

I still didn't get it, but it became a running joke all tour. I would make little jokes from stage about how I felt like a fish out of water on this tour. I was honestly just joking, I do love the Gungors. I was thinking about it throughout the three months we toured the country. We even made earth sandwich shirts . . . and I still didn't get it. It wasn't till after the whole tour was over that it clicked.

"OH! The earth made ITSELF a sandwich!"

It's wordplay: the bread is made of earth, the persons doing the experiment are also made of earth, and the sandwich itself is earth, thus the earth made ITSELF a sandwich.

The point, albeit, the most Gungorie way to get to it, is how silly we are to actually think humans are somehow not all just one thing. We see ourselves as sealed ecosystems, separate and autonomous from everything else around us. You, the tree, the ground, the bread, all its own thing. The truth is, not only at the molecular level but even in your bible, it's all earth. The bread, the metal of the device you might be reading or listening to this on, the paper you might be holding, the plastic of the chair you're sitting on, the wood of the frame of your home and the bolts that hold that wood together, and the people that built it all . . . it's all gathered dust of the earth. The earth made itself a sandwich.

YOU ARE MADE OF THE SOIL

"AYE N——— WHERE YOU FROM?!"!

My grandma touched down in Los Angeles during the early '60s because of the Watts Towers projects. Black families were allowed to own homes so it was a no-brainer. She and her slew of siblings began to make a new home in a state that has zero Jim Crow history. Her brothers, Uncle Billy Ray, Uncle Wayne, and Uncle CL, opted to stay below the southern part of the 110 freeway, in Watts and Compton. We didn't spend much time with them. Grandma was an Eastsider. The rest of the extended family's homes were a scatter plot between the spaces of Slauson on the northernmost side and Manchester on the southernmost, San Pedro on the easterly side, and Prairie on the west. Across the street from the Forum, home of our beloved Lakers. This is the soil I'm made of.

Grandma had been on 73rd and San Pedro since 1966. NeNe, my dad's sister, married the boy down the street. He becomes my uncle Sonny. The twins Dwayne and Dwight directly across the street from her. Madea's house, Uncle Sonny's mom, down the road closer to Main, right behind the Golden Ox burger joint. Larry and Bobby, four doors down. That Golden Ox burger joint on the corner of Florence and Main, oh man, the stories I could tell. The alleyway behind this home of the greasiest, most delicious legend of a burger was where I learned that I wasn't cut out for gang-banging, but that's a whole other story for a whole other chapter.

MUD

I can't keep my hand no clean
What is you complain fo'
Out if we come all yo' seeds
Dat what we been trainin fo'
We mud mud mud mud mud mud mud
Life and love come out my blood
Plant yo' seeds and grow yo' dreams.
blood bought mud blood it's all good

Adam and Eve was made of me!
What Genesis was picturing
Muck and mire of these hoods
Work yo' magic
Eat good.
Watch me push a rose or tree,
Right on through the concrete
Watch the sidewalk buckle rumble crumble right
*   below yo' feet.*
Mud dat where we comin from
Mud day where we goin' to
Dirty ugly funny buddy
What you thought dun fed yo' roots.
Mud. Mud
Don't just spin yo wheels my g cuz then you gon
*   get stuck stuck*
Member where you come from
People we are mud
Bring all yo blind yo sick yo hurt
Watch 'em mix that spit wit dirt
Tell that crowd to gather round
Simmer down then watch him work
Momma say he born that way
Never seen the night or day
Never seen the sun, moon, stars, trees, anything
Cash money hand rub
In between a lil mud
Bout to touch you no surprise

Bout to put this in yo eyes
Tell me now what you see
Men look like walkin trees
Touch again
What you see
Face of God lookin at me.
Humble beggar from the mud
All of y'all been judgin he
Definition irony that same mud healed he
We from the mud

It is of utmost importance to be able to navigate the neighborhoods in Los Angeles. And Google Maps will be of no service for you. You must be literate in graffiti. I am not at all kidding.

The 110 freeway, for the most part, divides the Eastside from the Westside. It was also the demarcation to where the neighborhoods turned from African American to Mexican.

The street names that ran north and south became shorthand for not only what part of town you are from but what color your shoelaces were. Figueroa, Hoover, Vermont, Western, Crenshaw, most likely your shoelaces were blue. Once you get past the Shaw you're moving into Inglewood territory in which shoelaces turn to red.

When you're five years old growing up in this

scene, there's no awareness that the houses were placed on blocks that would become places of legendary violence. No clue that the feeder high school, had you stayed with your grandmother, was the high school the Crip gang started in. The grand matriarch, Great-Grandmother Momma Winnie, stays on Hoover Street but you don't know it's THE HOOVER. You are just happy to enjoy the collard greens. To play with Sean, Qianna, and Devin in the backyard (she was insistent we stay in the backyard). There's a living history in these concrete blocks, in these meager wood and concrete houses that almost all have porches. The weather is too perfect to slap dominos on the inside. Plus someone gotta keep watch for the police.

Grandma lived on 73rd and San Pedro. Between San Pedro and Main. She would later move up to 67th between San Pedro and Avalon. Two blocks from Ramona's, THE GREATEST, and best-kept secret, taco in Los Angeles. This is the gray borderlands of Black and Latino neighborhoods. Avalon demarks the spot where all billboards and store signs turn to Spanish. On 73rd and on 67th, although they are bilingual, our laces were absolutely blue.

Here, the afternoon sun gives off a very specific hue of orange. In all the neighborhoods in all the parts of California I've lived in, the sun never looks quite like this. I suppose it's those iconic LA palm trees, mixed with jet fuel emissions from LAX, mixed with gun smoke, mixed with birria and carne asada, mixed with struggle, immigration, lowriders, and mariachi. Whatever it was, I'll never forget that color of the sun in the afternoon.

There's a narrative in the air, of bravery that comes out of Black excellence. There is the blown-up Black Panther office on 41st and Central that Pops attended. A future for the Normandie and Florence car wash that you took your uncle Sonny's Eldorado to every weekend that would become ground zero of the LA riots once puberty hit. Some timeless rap music is being birthed right in the backyard that butts up against your aunt Ethel's house on 64th and Vermont. You're clueless that your cousin is gonna go to high school with Nipsey, brother. He wasn't Nipsey then. He was just another kid from the 60s. He was just another kid in the Head Start reading program that your aunt NeNe worked at. What is for certain is there is something in the water here, the hose water just tastes different. The grocery store has a certain musicality to it. Somehow you are in love with a place. This is South Central Los Angeles.

LA got me making excuses for her.
She got issues but you don't know what we been
   through!
Three riots Crack attack
Pachuco vatos
You can't stay mad after biting that
King Taco

I didn't join our family's street gang. 73rd was the street my pops got stabbed in the stomach by his homie Bobby across the street. The hood where Pops and Uncle Ed beat the shit out of a guy who tried to cheat lil Eddy Petty in a pool game. Where Uncle Ed got slammed on the driveway by LAPD in front of my grandma. 73rd and San Pedro, where I got dropped off five days a week for child care for my first five years, where I saw my first heroin needle, first punch in the face, first drug deal. Where I heard Biz Markie and Kool Moe Dee for the first time. Where my roots are planted. The soil that all my narrative sprouts from. I didn't join, because I don't live there. That's my grandma's house. That's my dad's street. Not mine. By the time I was of age, I was twenty minutes east, in an all Mexican hood, run by the Mexican Mafia. I was in the San Gabriel Valley in a small hood called Valinda. Where yo' mamma pays rent is out of your hands; however, the way we are made, where she pays rent is of the utmost importance. 73rd and San Pedro courses through my veins, but I got mixed soil. I got San Gabriel Valley in my bones.

This little window was a greenhouse for me. The fact of the gang situation being almost exclusively Latino, the fact that I am not of pure South Central or Valinda blood, caused for different fruit to sprout out of the fertile soil of my soul. Instead, I became an artist. Ronnie Robles, Covina resident by way of Baldwin Park, birthplace of In-N-Out (you're welcome), northwest of my hood, a young man about five years my senior, put a can of spray paint in my hands.

Next door to the vatos
Potholes Tahoes.
Y'all know how the LA goes
Cops go bang in the name of the Law bro
Hoppin out with thangs that put holes in your
    jaw bones

That paint tapped me into rainbows, into the murals of my childhood. It tapped the imagination of those weekly car rides from 73rd and San

Pedro. Ronnie and I would drive through the intersection of the 10 and 101 freeway and in the back seat, I would be transfixed by the scene. It was the LA River. It can be a little confusing, but what makes the San Gabriel Valley separate from Los Angeles proper is the LA River. This paved river has a bunch of tributaries. The biggest one is the San Gabriel River. East of that river is this little enclave of cities, is where my bones begin to harden. North of Valinda, a sprawling suburb of West Covina. The home of one-fourth of the Black Eyed Peas. West Cov, La Puente, Valinda, City of Industry, city borders are blurry, again, unless you can read graffiti or speak Spanish. In which case, the borders were pretty simple.

And all over those paved sides of this massive storm drain of the LA River was the vibrant and living eyes of hip-hop. The graffiti world. It was the art school of my childhood. It was all the seeds my creative little heart needed. It was visually attached to the sounds coming out of Brenda and Patrick's garage. Next door to our humble Valinda home, where Patrick would practice with Junior and Oso their pop-locking. Where Thomas Pokinghorn, yes . . . Pokinghorn, the only white kid for miles, would teach me all the words to the Beastie Boys' song "Paul Revere." It was the first seed of what you all know as Propaganda.

AYE N——— WHERE YOU FROM?! This is gang talk. I'm being asked what my hood is. What color my shoelaces are. Deep in us all, we know, however, we are being asked so much more than that. Someone wants to know what I am made of. What's the crucible that forged me? Can I handle pressure, or am I fragile? Am I iron or wood, trees or flowers? Do I know my roots, and are they strong and deep? Can I handle the storm and winds? Did I survive anything? Did my mamma and daddy survive anything? Can I get pushed over if someone wanted me to fall?

Where I'm from, geography can answer that. Obviously people are far more complex than this, and it's insultingly reductive to use this as the only grid of understanding people. But the mud that you are made of does communicate a little bit about your alchemy. You from the sticks of Appalachia? That tells me you are most likely very resourceful. The elements don't scare you. Are you from the grit of motor city Detroit? That tells me that hard work is in your DNA. You worked for every penny you got and don't understand when people don't work! Calabasas? Say no more. Most likely you exist in a world of excess and decadence very few of us can relate to. I place no judgment good or bad on that, it just helps me navigate my interactions with you.

The soil gets in your bones. The soil makes your bones. Good, bad, and ugly, don't you ever discount your soil. Redeem it. It's sacred. There were a lot of people who made me who I am. But none more influential than those in South Central and Valinda. I am made of them.

I am made of planet
Oceans and stardust, not that far
From us
My skin's geology got its scars from us
Pain rivers eroded chasms and depressions
Made of cliff divers, and the rocks they stand on.
The abuse of man and beast, made his resources
*   increase.*
I come from the least.
We make treasure out of trash.
And understand the land in a way that came
*   from pain.*
Your loss my gain in the end it's not equal
I appeal to the resilience of my people
I remain calm and watch nations rage.
I've seen oceans part by the ancient days.

THE SOIL SPEAKS

I've recently had the opportunity to travel internationally more than I ever have before. Notably, I knocked out two bucket-list locations: 1. Israel and Palestine (man, that's a mess over there; so glad I'm not the one tasked to try to solve it!) and 2. Ethiopia. Since I have a Christian worldview, visiting Israel should inspire huge tingly feels. We've been reading about these places in our bibles since kindergarten. But I'm also a Californian so these places feel as real as Middle Earth, or Narnia, or Wakanda . . . well, maybe not Wakanda . . . that's a real place. Right? I digress.

(However, since I'm already digressing, I've often wondered why these fantasy worlds such as Middle Earth had fairies, elves, and dwarfs but no brown skin?! At least the seven kingdoms in GOT had Dornish Arabs and the Dothraki were clearly North African, albeit with a crazy white savior complex, but still. Apparently, the future doesn't have Black people either, according to every fantasy, science fiction, or future-focused movie I saw as a child. Anyway, I'm way off the rails here now.)

The point is that the places of scripture didn't seem real to me until I stood in them. The archaeology of the Holy Land is undeniable. My wife and I even celebrated our ten-year anniversary with a double baptism in the Jordan River. This was one of the most beautiful moments of my life. Standing in Caesarea, on the home of Tiberius, my soul leaped in me when we pulled into Galilee and I thought to myself, *This is Jesus's hood. I am shooketh!*

Ethiopia hit me much differently. The air, the coffee, the faith, the land, all of it yelled at me, "You will always matter."

NATURE MIGHT SNITCH

If the wind whistles
And the water babbles
And the trees keep score in their rings
If birds carry stories in the matter of pollen
The elders say
Hills have eyes
If that's so, we better pray they not snitches.

Maybe our forefathers thought all the food,
All the goodies were for us
Momma goes to the sto erry two weeks
It's magic, I open the savannas as pantry cabinets
  and food is plentiful
What sorcery is provisions
Medicine sprouts out the ground as flowers and
  leaves that we did nothing to produce

Maybe we started choppin down the trees to shut
them up.
Maybe our ancestors had a sense that mamma
finna be pissed
If these rolling hills breathe one word to Earth.
We better pray they not snitches.
Maybe we scared that lil bro bison was gonna tell
mom we playing too rough
Maybe we wiped out our siblings because we were
scared she was finna ground us
The elders say hills have eyes
If that's so, we better pray they not snitches.
Because if ever Mamma find out what we dun did
to her house. . . .

I've been mistaken for an Ethiopian my whole life and that brings up a gumbo of emotions that really only other Black American slave descendants can understand. I'm not here to play the oppression Olympics because no one wins in that game; however, some uniqueness about our experience must be acknowledged. For Black people, it's not as simple as 23andMe, which for some people is a rad modern invention. But it's not that simple for us. It's a reclaiming of what was stolen. A redemption that's almost impossible to put into words.

Allow me to make a case here. My indigenous brothers and sisters saw their land taken, customs outlawed, and languages erased. Even with all this suffering and tragedy, if I'm honest, some part of me is envious of the indigenous in this country. They can name their tribes, and somehow, the sacred flame of their souls was not completely quenched. Against all odds, their traditions have been preserved. I marvel at the fortitude of spirit when I visit the rez.

My Jewish brothers and sisters went from being ruled by Canaanites, Egyptians, Babylonians, Assyrians, Persians, Greeks, and Romans, who, for sheer purpose of shade, changed the name of the region to Palestine, in reference to the Philistines, then by Byzantinians, early Muslims, Christian crusaders, Mamluks, Ottomans, and the British, then they endured the Holocaust, for crying out loud. Talk about collective trauma; it goes back five millennia! Somehow, miraculously, they practice the same songs, customs, and rituals set forth in the Bronze Age!

I also envy my wife who, as a first-generation Mexican American, knows her mother language. We've touched soil in the place of her actual ancestors and ate food that her foremothers planted.

For those of us who are slave descendants though, even with a DNA test, your best guess is which tribes shared a boat ride to North America, or to which plantation y'all were sold. For us, our loss of heritage is not just a result that comes from migration; it's more purposeful and systematic. It's the Willie Lynch theory in full effect—the idea of setting slaves against one another in order to control them. Break that African man's spirit! Rape his wife and make him watch so he knows he's powerless. Make him fight his fellow slaves for the master's entertainment. Make him jealous of those light-skinned house slaves. Make him hate himself and see his own homeland as savage and uncivilized. In time, his only tie to his roots is a plantation in Mississippi. Over decades and centuries, we have been told, "You are NOT a people group with a long rich history. You're property and you should be thankful we gave you a bible, and even had the wisdom to build into our documents the chance for you to have rights. Be thankful that we pulled you from loincloths and cannibalism."

What if America takes a page from post–World War II Europe and starts drawing new national lines based on ethnicity (which is just as ridiculous and impossible biologically and politically now as it was then). Where y'all sending Black people? Africa? Where in Africa? Marcus Garvey tried going back in the Back-to-Africa movement of the 1920s. Liberia or Sierra Leone, in the nineteenth century? None of these places has been the same since. What do you do when you're not wanted where you are but have no place to go? Should we just point at a part of Africa and drop ourselves in a nation? Take a look at modern-day Israel . . . tell me how well that tactic works.

We are who we are. We are Black and we are American. We are Black Americans.

Yet somehow, when I'd meet a brother or sister from Ethiopia, they would just start speaking their native tongue, as if I would understand, and then, they'd get upset with me when I couldn't speak it back to them. I let them down as a Habesha who doesn't know his roots. Forgotten his home. Became too American.

So a couple years ago, when I touched ground in Addis Ababa, I was not shocked that the guard at the airport didn't even check my passport. Or, while dining at our hotel's restaurant downtown enjoying some Doro Wat, the waiter looked to me to translate for the group. No surprise when in every direction I look I see a doppelgänger of one of my relatives. It's very disorienting to feel at home in a place you've never been. It feels like a divine hand is reaching through centuries and whispering: "Prop, I know who you are. Despite suffering, pain, loss, oppression, and genocide, you are made of sacred soil, and it shows. You are made of the first Christian city, of the provable tribe of Israel, of the soil that gave the world coffee. You are made of the richest of spirits. You are now standing in your biological and spiritual home. That soil is sacred. And you are made of it. Don't you ever forget."

The next time you feel like you aren't enough,

you've lost too much, or your identity is gone—
buried in an ash heap of insignificance and
suffering—please, for me, slow down, look at your
cheekbones, your freckles, and take a breath. Re-
member that the weight of the world could col-
lapse your chest but somehow the spirit fills your
lungs and pushes back that gravity of life. Think
of your hometown, or the bullies who picked on
you, or the third-grade teacher who told you that
you sucked at fractions (I hated that lady). Exam-
ine your wrinkles, flaws, and stretch marks, for
they are your trophies. Let your body testify, your
ancestors yell, and your God prove to you the
truth that you are a masterpiece.

THE SOIL IS SACRED +
THE SOIL IS A GIFT + YOU
HAVE ALWAYS BEEN ONE
WITH THE SOIL + YOU ARE
MADE OF THE SOIL =
YOU ARE A SACRED GIFT

SACRED FEMININE

My queen our flag. Made of the toughest of rawhide.
A story of glory and grit,
Sunburnt, weatherworn, potholed concrete,

Arteries pump like the traffic of our streets.
The rarest of ovaries
All hovering over me
Our feet city our Heartbeat
It's all her
She is made of mother.
The opulence of soil that gave us chocolate
Take off ya chanclas
Borders are not real, you standing on sacred
    ground
She got royalty loyalty, inside her DNA
Her soil mapped the stars before any of ours
She got drops of middle passage
Sprinkles of West African
Ivory Costa Chica what's happenin
She's a wee bit, brilliant.
Refer to her by her prefix.
A PhD checkin steps on her WeFit
Seasons don't shake her she is spicy tajín,
Sprinkled on the strongest of Mayan Maize.
A strawberry field glimmering in the summer sun
loca where you coming from?
East Los, HP, Acapulco, Highland Park, Boyle
    Heights.
Made of south LA, Atlantic and Florence
With the hustle of the street vendor. Everybody
    needs yea
Ladies and gentlemen
Sacred Feminine

I AM HERE

I am fixed point on the horizon,
I am North Star in the fight against the forces that
   gentrify us.
I am keeper for the flame
I am tattoo
Birthmark
Birth certificate
Hood pass.
Self-addressed envelope.
I am 3rd-grade teacher that ruined a love of math
Fractions destroyed us all
I am reminder
I am corner store
First misdemeanor
First kiss
Senior ditch day
I am safe place and trauma source
Baggage and glory days
I am memories rose-colored and bruised purple
Daffodils
Overdue
Forgotten lunch money
Sending you forget-me-nots
I am stomach knots
Grounded
Punishment
I am Tito pico,

64th and Vermont
A block from Gage and Hoover
I am 15 and Millikin
Amar and Azusa
I am pavement gum
The Saltwater that seasons the night air
On the sidewalk the OG in the
Wheelchair yellin hit a left right there.
Ramen noodle fusion
Collard greens
Dumplings
Boca del Río
Surfboards
Sunscreen
I am poetry, poverty, prosperity, melancholy
   and holiday.
I am home
You are the welcomed

TERRAFORMING
PROJECT 4

1. **PLANT A VEGETABLE!** Legit just one. I
know this is the *most* city-boy thing ever.
But it is the best way to tangibly get your
hands dirty in some soil. Even if you are
a regular gardener, try doing it with the

mind-set of how magical the ground is. A
seed becomes food. Wow!

2. HANG UP A WORLD MAP. Hang it
somewhere in your home, but use one
without nation borders. If you really 'bout
it, see if you can find a Dymaxion map,
which is a projection of a world map that
can be unfolded and flattened to two
dimensions. It's a whole other way to view
the world on a flat surface. What's gonna
blow your mind is how all the land on Earth
is connected.

I actually have both a geographic version
and one without borders. I often just sit
and imagine the places on the map. When
I first started touring I used to put blue X's
on cities and places I wanted to perform
in and red X's on places I have performed;
I watched it fill up over the years. This
practice made me think way more globally,
made me remember just how connected we
all are. Figure out your own daydreaming
ritual with your maps.

3. EXPLORE YOUR CITY WITHOUT
USING GOOGLE MAPS. Then, let
yourself try to figure out how to get back
home. Or maybe take a different route on

your morning commute, take it slow and appreciate the beautiful scenery, the nature or urban decay. Notice how the trees and hills led the engineers on how to and where to lay the pavement.

4. DO SOME RESEARCH ON LOCAL NATIVE TRIBES. Find out what native tribe was originally on the land you live on or grew up in. Learn a little about them, their customs, history, and ways of life. For the Americas, New Zealand, and Australia, you can go to https://native-land.ca/. It's an interactive map that shows you what tribal lands you might live on. You can click your area and learn about that tribe. Most Native American and Canadian tribes have tribal meetings, so you could reach out and sit in on one of their meetings if that is allowed. Some tribes are not really keen on this, which we respect, but they might have a museum or cultural center and you can see if they offer a tour. Get involved with helping them in some way.

5. DO A LAND ACKNOWLEDGMENT. I learned from my time with tribes to do a thing called a Land Acknowledgment. It's about taking a second and honoring in your

mind and heart the people that came before you and are buried on the land you stand on, where crops grew and life was given so you can stand where you are. If you're so inclined, thank the Creator for those things you had no hand in, but have given you so much.

6. DO A GROUNDING EXERCISE. This is something Alma does that I'm not so much into, but she says it's superhelpful. Whenever she's visiting a new natural setting, such as a campsite, beach, hiking trail, or foreign country, she takes a few minutes to take off her shoes and socks and plant her feet on that ground. She takes a few deep breaths to feel the warmth of that ground. It makes her feel much more connected to that place and recognizes the gift it is. I personally have a disdain for the feeling of being barefoot unless it's at the beach. However Alma loves being barefoot, and she's a better person than me so always default to her advice rather than mine.

THE PEOPLE

INSTITUTIONAL NEIGHBORLINESS

Sometimes I imagine trees in therapy.
In utter shambles as to why the mammals
work against themselves.

FEEL TOO MUCH

The healing
The feeling of all the feels
I want to feel too much
I need to feel too much
Sweet Jesus
Seeking the feeling of all the feels
Help me feel helpless
To see my neediness as a gift which transforms me to
   advocate
Help me see me in even the eyes of my enemies,
Help me not to hold back tears for fear of being
   called girly.
And toss all the toxic notions into the furthest ocean
   of obnoxious.
Since the best of us that ever lived was marked by
   tenderness
Remind me they are me.
Help me to know too much to be okay and not
   enough to be at peace.
Help me love hard and fast and deep
And with no need for qualifiers
And thus the gentleness of words and touch is
   precisely because
I feel too much.

Before any poetry, listen I ain't a biter. I first heard this phrase, institutional neighborliness, from my homegirl Nish Weiseth. It was so packed with power that it inspired all this poetry.

This will most likely be the most Bible-ie chapter of this book so for you progressives, don't get triggered. To my theoBROgians, find comfort. The rest y'all . . . ignore this sentence.

If our neighbors are the people who live around us (whether physically or metaphorically), before we get into what it looks like to be a neighbor, we need to understand the places where we live. I can't stress this enough: WE ARE NOT CLOSED OFF FROM EACH OTHER. We all are connected. The world you live in can either flourish at the expense of others, or flourish WITH others. If you chose the former way, just know that one day, that cost will come out of your wallet and not your neighbors'. For our terraforming project, I'm suggesting that we should pursue the latter. The former way has a name, it's called building an *empire*, and a cursory survey of history will show you, we have done this for millennia and it has been a destructive force in our societies.

That's a good place to start. Let's take a good hard look at empires past and present.

I hope your words have a curfew.

THE LANGUAGE
OF THE EMPIRE

In the Bible, Paul was a master of reading the culture. A crap ton of Paul's writings pull from and make reference to his contemporary culture. He would be referring to stuff that the readers of his letters would immediately recognize without any need for him to add extra commentary. Just like if I were to say "the force was strong with Paul," I most likely wouldn't have to say "you see what I did there?!" (Even using the phrase, "you see what I did there" is itself a pop culture reference that I'm sure you caught immediately.)

One example is his treatise on the "body of Christ" in Corinthians. That imagery is not out of nowhere. The average Roman citizen understood that Rome, the empire, was one living being. Each person made up a part of it, only some parts were worthy of honor and others weren't. Paul was bouncing off that concept and sayin, "Yo! WE are one, only in the body of Christ; *unlike Rome*, each part is as important as the other, AND we have a duty to honor those parts that aren't given the shine or respect they should. See, empire says one thing. *Kingdom* says something totally different. And though the empire might be made of you, that doesn't mean the empire made you."

HOME?

It came on a Sunday
Hazy and draped in irony.
It darkens the horizons.
Akin to white men touching down on Incan
  shores.
Akin to the Babylonian king knocking on
  Daniel's door
Home is no longer home.
You could take the wings of the morning
Attempt to fly where?
When your wings are now subleased and someone
  has bought the air.
We are just trying to feed our kids.
And you could chant down the occupier
But the empire always strikes back.
You could try to set the forest fire
But how will you get your home back
When your whole home is in crisis?
But what's the price you pay when the home
  prices have priced you out of house and home?
Where is here?
What is home?
Somewhere between citizen prisoner and refugee.
We ain't cross the border, boy the border
  crossed we.

THE EFFECT
OF THE EMPIRE

"Aye, homie, I just work here, I ain't from here!"
If I were to synthesize and translate the first few
chapters of the book of Daniel, it would basically be
that. In my estimation, Daniel, which, according
to the text, ain't even his name anymore, a point
we will come back to later, is the closest parallel to
the life I've attempted to live. That is a super-self-
aggrandizing statement, I'm fully aware. However,
let me explain by looking closer at what's happen-
ing historically, geopolitically, and socioculturally
to big homie Daniel.

There are many ways to conquer and expand an
empire. You can go the scorched earth route: just
go in and strong-arm everyone. Kill 'em all, burn
the ashes, rape the women, and start over with your
own people. Another way is to be the "New Sher-
iff": pull up and overpower the rulers and place
yourself in charge. The people's lives don't neces-
sarily change, they just have a new leader and hope
that this new guy is kinder than the last. Sort of
like how America got the Philippines . . . oh, you
didn't know that the Philippines was an Amer-
ican colony for a sec? Oof. Ouch, too real. And
finally, and to me the most cunning way: assimi-
late into submission. This was Babylon's approach.

The assimilation approach creates a monolithic culture by slowly erasing distinctions. The empire says, look, you can keep your faith and traditions, as long as they stay indoors. You can keep your jobs, just pay tribute to us. As a matter of fact, let us meet your best and brightest, have them come work for us, we will give them a great education, good jobs, we will treat them like our own. It will be great!

So the lead thinkers of the conquered get trained in the ways of the conqueror, treated so well that they might almost forget that they are slaves to this empire. Sometimes that politeness can lull you to sleep. It makes you forget that these people don't love y'all. Well, they love y'all, but in the way that a person loves their new car and keeps it nice and clean with all its maintenance scheduled out perfectly.

Eventually these leaders who get trained by the empire begin to adopt the ways of the empire, take on the traditions of the empire, and see the empire's ways as better than their own ways. They begin to feel as though *this* is the way forward for our people, even encouraging the rest to come along with them. Pretty soon they take on the names the empire gives them. It begins to somewhat turn their stomach to see their own people behaving so barbaric, so primitive. "Listen, we are Babylonians now, stop acting so ancient." Black people have a term for this . . . House n———s. During the chattel slavery era of America, the house slaves were usually a little more fair-skinned (most likely products of rape at the hands of the white masters to the Black slave women), and much less worn from working the fields in the hot Southern sun. They were well-fed, well-spoken, and very clean. And some, if they weren't careful, could forget that they were just property. They began to look down a little bit on the field n———s, who were darker, rougher, underfed with leftover pig slop, and calloused from sixteen to seventeen hours of manual labor. House n———s kept the field n———s in check.

Step back into Belteshazzar's world. Yeah, his name ain't Daniel anymore. He and his homies were given Babylonian names. Names fashioned in the image of the empire. Here's the thing, if you come from a Judeo-Christian background, you might be led to see the Israelites as main characters. History tells a different story. They are nobodies. They are nomads, former Egyptian slaves who wandered the desert getting into tribal skirmishes while the rest of the world was discovering geometry, inventing irrigation, and building five of the seven wonders of the world.

Think of it like this. During the time of World War II, can you tell me some of the names and/or events that happened in the tribal wars of Northern Siberia? Yeah, me neither. No disrespect to Northern Siberia, I'm just sayin the history camera wasn't focused up there. Are you today years old when you learned right before World War II, Spain was in a civil war? Same energy with ancient Israel. They were just another conquered people. Sure, they had a high watermark with King David and Solomon, but that was literally five hundred years before Daniel's time. Belteshazzar and the rest of Israel were further away from David and Solomon than we are from the signing of the Declaration of Independence. We weren't even a country five hundred years ago. The Protestant Reformation was around five hundred years ago. That's how long ago we talkin.

We are talking about a people that don't know who they are anymore. All they know is this: conquered! The perfect cultural moment for Babylon to do its thing. It's also this group of Israelis that decide they need to figure out who they are, so they compile the Torah to remember who they really are, to get back into their collective memory the legacy of Moses, Abraham, and David. To remember that they are not just tools in an empire, they are more than their circumstances, to keep the metaphor going, to remember that, no matter how good they treat him,

Belteshazzar is his slave name, his given name is Daniel.

So here is the moment, where the empire pulled the best and brightest to place in the care of their own palaces. Learning alongside the sons of royalty, to be fed well and placed in leadership. Daniel makes moves that would seem odd to the modern-day evangelical. The evangelical—well, let me be specific, the white Western evangelical, and let me be even more specific, white Western evangelical as a social construct, and white not as ethnicity but as white-ness, evangelical not as faith but subcultural demographic—this person tends to take the opt-out approach. Almost as if the solution to an evil empire is to build their own version of empire. Christian schools, coffee shops, health insurance, chicken sandwiches, music, festivals, you name it, there's a Christian version. If you work it right, you could go through an entire day and never be in contact with any non-Christian person or business. Thing is, that's just not what Daniel did. He stayed at the palace, he let them call him Belteshazzar, he worked for Babylon, and he succeeded. Not like kinda succeeded, he was THE BEST employee they had. So much so that when Babylon fell, his references were so good that the next empire hired him! He had to have made the king tons of money. He didn't opt out. He stayed in. The antidote to empire isn't another empire, it's kingdom.

"Aye, I just work here, I ain't from here," shouts Daniel. He should get that mug tattooed on his neck! "I'm not gonna eat the empire's food, but I'll do the work, to show you I'm not made of what makes you, I'm cut from something else. Look, y'all can call me whatever you want, that name is made of the empire's image. I'm not from here. I'm from a different kingdom. My code is different. I move different"; he's basically an ancient Nipsey Hussle shouting, "I ain't nothin like you fucc'in rap n———s!"

So when the empire makes a graven statue in the image of its king, and it expects the subjects to bow to the image, Daniel makes it real clear, "Bruh, I just work here, I didn't eat what you feeding me, literally and metaphorically. Empire only begets empire. Thus I'm not fashioned in your image."

Let me bake your noodles. Jesus brought that same energy to the empire of his time, Rome! I know this because when the Pharisees say to him, "Should the Jews pay taxes?" it was a trap. Because if Jesus says don't pay taxes, he is inciting law-breaking, if he says pay it, then he is a sellout!

But Jeshua says, "Show me the money, breh. Whose IMAGE is on this coin?" (he didn't say "breh" but you get it). Well, the answer is Caesar. So the coin and, in turn, that economic system and philosophy is made in the image of the empire. "It's theirs, give them what's theirs." Then he says, "Give to God what belongs to God." The inference is what image are YOU made in? He's saying you are made in the image of God, thus you give yourself to your kingdom. MY BOY! I JUST WORK IN ROME! I AIN'T FROM ROME!

Are you gon make me list,
How many descriptions I have fit?
How many hashtags made me scream
Cuz, that could be me?

WE AIN'T HAVE NOTHIN

System kills our prophets and mocks our mourn
  for em.
Gives us balls and mics and demands we perform
  for em.
Crazy
What three hundred years have been tryin to say
  to you
Why I gotta explain it ain't plain to you?

We ain't have nothin. But nothing is sufficient
Kept my belly full of the stuff the rich is missing.
Y'all could grow a little if your little minds can
*   listen*
Privilege you protect has made you a victim
Crazy

You think you blameless I know you Shameless,
You can't even see the pain in our faces.
Ain't got a frame for the effects of displacement
Now marvel at the joy that comes from our spaces
Let me learn you what nothing can do.

WAYS OF THE EMPIRE

In this world we are building, we ain't made in the image of empire! Empire functions on scarcity, which looks like, *Well, there's only so many resources to go around, so I need to get as much as I can for me and mine. It's not that I actively hate anyone else, it's that I have higher priority for my well-being than yours.* The empire builds walls to keep THEM away from us, because THEM just want our stuff. Empire stratifies society based on what they can produce for us. The more you can make me, the more important you are. Empire is always attempting to self-replicate but not out of care but out of a desire to keep expanding its borders. My G, the answer to empire is not more empire.

Empire is what happened to the generations following Adam and Eve in your bible. Immediately after the Fall, humans somehow decided some of them were more important than others. They immediately built up ziggurats to reach the heavens. (Side note, ziggurats were these tall mud-brick monuments that the ancient Assyrians built. They kinda look like narrow skyscrapers.) They built empires. Empires choose who is more worthy of its recognition and resources.

I don't want to function on scarcity models because that forces me to make a value judgment about the importance of another human's life. I'm tryin to live with the plenty model. Look, I'm from LA. When the ice cream truck pulls up, if I got money, we ALL eating! If Ronnie McNutt who lived across the street got a new video game, we ALL got a new game.

We don't build walls because walls mean fear, and I don't fear my neighbor because I'm on some YEAH THEM TOO. My neighbor is only dangerous if they follow empire rules. If they are afraid that there's not enough to go around, they might think their best bet is to take from me. But if my neighbor knows that all my purchases, all my possessions are for all us to flourish, and all their possessions are also for all of us, what is the point in stealing? What's the point of hoarding?

Here is where you get frustrated with me, right? *This is some superidealistic, not possible, imaginary world you are living in!* You're right. This book is about making up a world! I'm challenging you to have an unfettered imagination! We are terraforming here! But, yes, the next question is how can we do this practically?! I don't know!

I do know that Jesus talked about the possibility. Dropping gems like "consider the birds," all Jesus talked about was the Kingdom! Bringing about a new way of living despite the comings and goings of empires. I'm literally ripping these ideas off from the parables of the gospels.

I'm trying to build a world where people don't have to find identity through collective suffering. Where the stories that make you are marred or erased by the Visigoth that is empire. A world in which my greatest interest is using who I am to see others flourish!

Turns out we are more connected than we want to admit.

Y'ALLS MONSTER

What a strange relationship y'all have with us
  monsters,
For a world that is in the business of hunting us
  down,
Murdering our kind you sure seem to enjoy
  conjuring us up out of your own unprocessed
  consciences.
Your phrases confuse us all the time.
You know what phrase I hate the most?
It feeds the worst of our kind
"The Media"
I don't even know what's wrong with y'all?!
Y'all speak of this "media" guy but I've never
  seen him in any of my closets, or under beds
I don't recognize this monster,
IT
don't live in forests, or tundras
Or lake beds with Tia LLORONA
Or dodging aswang
But I've done my homework and I'm a little
  confused
. . . There is no "THE" media.
That would be "the mediUM"
Ain't this y'alls language?
As if that which is already plural is a singular
  sentient entity with self-awareness.

As if THE media,
The plural that is singular,
Is not conjured up, funded, distributed and
consumed by you.
There is ONE media?
The media
The plural that is singular, right?
And it is an
IT?
Maybe I've done too many monster mashes and
have a papier-mâché brain
Y'all say "the" media is content and the roads for
which it travels on?
Earthlings are a strange thing. I should stick to
eating kids, right?
Just stay in the closet next to y'alls' skeletons.
Wait, so car is vehicle AND person driving
AND destination?
How?
How you blame paper for the words on it?
How you blame internet for website?
Which came first? Your binary thinking or your
binary code?
Shame on Google Maps for driving your spouse
to the rooftop of our humble homes under side
peace sleeping quarters.
The map is a monster
THE media

The plural that is singular, right?
IT
has an agenda,
ITS
agenda is beneficial or dire based on what YOU
  think is beneficial or dire
IT
has its own plans to steal your kids, affirm
  LGBTQ lifestyles AND turn y'all into
  libtards
IT
is evil
IT
Sound to me like
IT
sounds a lot like you
BUT IT
is the monster tho
Am I gettin it?
IT'S
brainwashing huh?
IT
is the problem because
IT
speaks for THEM
And we all know THEM IS EVIL
What a monster
I wonder why

IT

don't sound like and look or feel familiar

THE *media*

The plural that is singular, right?

IT'S

wearing a YOU *coat*

What a monster, right?

This monster don't look like us

Media ain't from round here

This monster from your hood

Media from your mouth

Slowly shoots its tentacles out your mouth at
    every dinner table when asked how was
    your day

Slithers its snail-like slime lines at 5G speeds
    every time you click send

I don't think that

IT

is a monster at all, or even an

IT

It's all in your head. Hmm, maybe that's why I
    ain't seen him in my hood.

DOES ANYBODY KNOW WHAT'S GOING ON OUTSIDE?!

The greatest threat to freedom they say is
  harboring terrorists.
As if Syria's a monolith.
I seen down the street these four men from ISIS
  drag the homie granny by her hair to the street.
They said, "Give us your sons!"
but it sounds worse in Arabic. She was so
  confused, her family Pashtun
It was that day we found out we lived inside a
  Caliphate.
This is bull's-eye for the targeted air strikes; the air
  might have a slight scent of sulfur.
You get used to it.
Blown-out windows on the bus of my morning
  commute
Leftover land mines, better take another route
This is not my Islam
Why should I remain calm?
Do the worst of your preachers teach us right about
  your Jesus?
Where's your empathy?
How come you can't see me?
How did my house become your enemy?
In come the US troops. I'm supposed to trust you?
You on my side, like I ain't never seen the news?
You look at them fools and think that's what
  Muslims do?

At least when you step inside my house take off
yo shoes?!
How am I supposed to choose?
I was born in a war. I have seen the darkest of the
hearts of men
And I was only ten.

ICPTSD (INNER-CITY PTSD)

Who are you to judge us,
You never lived among us
You know what shootin kites is?
Then you should keep ya mouth shut
Gorillas wilding Racial profiling.
Sometimes the biggest fight is to not prove
you right.
And how do you know what's right?
Your codes of conduct? Please?
Your monopolies of corporate greed then got the
nerve to call us thieves
We are not so different. Your product is addictive
and we just wanna fit in!
Feel the longing the sense of belonging the broken
seeds of Maslow's hierarchy of needs
The need to be needed we ain't so different
at some point,

every boy wanna be just like his daddy
At one point,
he was Hercules, a mystery or absentee
at some point
We saw the city was doin the fathering
And IMMA be just like it.
Imma bleed blue and breathe smog. Run numbers
    it's the best odds
Inner-city PTSD kinda like a war vet. Except
    P stands for present
Who are you to judge us.
You don't live among us
Your mortgage underwater too?
Then you should keep your mouth shut.
Schools are failing.
War on drugs.
Pathways to prison
Wasn't born thugs
Who are you to judge us.
You don't live among us
By any means, you living above your means
Who are you to judge us
Get jumped for ya Jumpmans and walk the
    same street tomorrow that's the only way to
    school. You got shoes I could borrow?
When John Perez tio put him on Valinda flats,
    he let his cousin break his jaw then went and
    got matching tatts

These are our rites of passages, inner-city bar
   mitzvah
You're officially a man. Which means, you're
   expected by any and all means to respect the
   clan you came from and put first the team.
I know you understand this.
The code exists on every college campus.
And in the halls of Congress
We ain't so different. You just like me.
Y'all call them political parties.
Who are you to judge us,
You never lived among us
You know what shootin kites is?
Then you should keep ya mouth shut

COMMUNITY
OVER EMPIRE

I'd be a full-blown Libertarian, total free market economy guy, if it wasn't for racism. What a statement, can't believe I just let myself write it. I'm the child of a Black Panther, which I know, they were communist for the most part, but growing up in that kind of home, we learned that we will never see justice in this land. The United States was not formed for the flourishing of "all" people, seeing as how every people group other than wealthy white males had some moment where they had to fight to be included in the Constitution.

We aren't leaving, we shed blood to build this place, for free I might add. It's just as much mine as it is anyone else's. Black people, and by extension anyone who had to fight to be included in the Constitution, can't get justice from the system so we must find it on our own. The problem is that when we say "justice," we often have totally different ideas of what it means. In Harvard law professor Michael Sandel's book *Justice*, he presents justice as falling into three categories: theories based on (1) "maximizing welfare," (2) "respecting freedom," and (3) "promoting virtue." Let's take a minute to unpack each one.[1]

Category one, "Maximizing welfare," Sandel explains, is the liberal, left-wing, big government view of justice. It asks: What's the most good for the greatest number of people? What makes things fair? That is justice. Everyone gets the best possible shot. This may not include *everyone* but as many people as we can.

Category 2, "Respecting freedom," is the Libertarian view. Basically, let me make my own decisions. I'm a decent human, I don't need someone to tell me that I should help my neighbor, of course I don't want them to die! I want them to succeed. If my neighbor has everything they need then that also secures my own safety. I know me best, and I will treat others the way I want to be treated. I am going to do what I need to do to ensure my success and you should too.

Category three, "Promoting virtue," is the conservative, right-wing's view of justice. It's interested in doing whatever is the "right" thing, which amounts to justice. We all should pursue decency and good and that is what the law should produce. Good is something that is not relative, it is transcendent, its source is above us. Virtue is upstream from politics so we should pursue virtue.

Of course, these are theoretical positions so odds are we all have a little bit of each of these categories in us. We all want to see good in the world, we don't want to see people suffer, and we really wish people would stay out of our business. If I want to open a coffee shop, and it flops, let it flop because I was a sucky businessman, not because of some zoning law that just serves the wealthy. I've built a rap career. If it succeeds, let it succeed because y'all really rocked with me. If it fails, it fails because my music isn't good, not because of some algorithm that favors mumble rap.

In the world I wanna build, I'd love to see all three of these things meld into one. I can't really be Libertarian because I live in a world where racism is cooked into the fabric of our society. It's baked into the laws, and every right I have in this nation has come from the government intervening into the affairs of its citizens. I can't be a free market economist because the market is just coded speech for people, and if people decide they don't want Black families in their neighborhood, then they will figure out a way to zone their cities so that they don't have to sell to me. Side note, that happened, it's called redlining.

But how could I actually work to meld those three together? Let's explore that together next.

Turns out connection isn't knowing another,
it's the process of another showing themself
Intimacy returns the favor

DAG, FAM, JUST LOVE YOUR NEIGHBOR

If we're looking for a better definition of justice, I'm going to suggest we use "institutional neighborliness," which, again, is a phrase I got from my homegirl Nish Weiseth. The idea is, if in my heart I believe humans have inalienable value, that my flourishing is connected to theirs, or for those of us who profess some affinity to the teaching of Jesus who says the greatest commandment is to love God and neighbor, then the most efficient and highest potential of impact is in the voting booth. Vote with the good of others in mind. Let's make laws that consider the good of our neighbor. Nish nailed it! I don't think I can state this any better than her. Also, sweet brother Dr. Martin Luther King Jr. in his vision gave us twenty-five characteristics of what he calls the Beloved Community as written by Dr. Arthur Wright, which is the perfect example of what "institutional neighborliness" looks like:

1. Offers radical hospitality to everyone; an inclusive family rather than exclusive club;

2. Recognizes and honors the image of God in every human being;

3. Exhibits personal authenticity, true respect, and validation of others;

4. Recognition and affirmation, not eradication, of differences;

5. Listens emotionally (i.e., with the heart)—fosters empathy and compassion for others;

6. Tolerates ambiguity—realizes that sometimes a clear-cut answer is not readily available;

7. Builds increasing levels of trust and works to avoid fear of difference and others;

8. Acknowledges limitations, lack of knowledge, or understanding—and seeks to learn;

9. Acknowledges conflict or pain in order to work on difficult issues;

10. Speaks truth in love, always considering ways to be compassionate with one another;

11. Avoids physical aggression and verbal abuse;

12. Resolves conflicts peacefully, without violence, recognizing that peacefully doesn't always mean comfortably for everybody;

13. Releases resentment and bitterness through self-purification (i.e., avoidance of internal violence through spiritual, physical, and psychological care);

14. Focuses energy on removing evil forces (unjust systems), not destroying persons;

15. Unyielding persistence and unwavering commitment to justice;

16. Achieves friendship and understanding through negotiation, compromise, or

consensus——considering each circumstance
to discern which will be most helpful;

17. Righteously opposes and takes direct action
against poverty, hunger, and homelessness;

18. Advocates thoroughgoing, extensive
neighborhood revitalization without
displacement (this also applies to the
church—working toward responsible and
equitable growth, discipleship, and worship);

19. Blends faith and action to generate a
commitment to defeating injustice (not
forgetting that injustice can also be found
within the church);

20. Encourages and embraces artistic expressions
of faith from diverse perspectives;

21. Fosters dynamic and active spirituality—
recognizes that we serve a dynamic God
who is not left behind by a changing world
or people, and that a passive approach will
not work;

22. Gathers together regularly for table
fellowship, and meets the needs of everyone
in the community;

23. Relies on scripture reading, prayer, and
corporate worship for inner strength;

24. Promotes human rights and works to create a nonracist society;

25. Shares power and acknowledges the inescapable network of mutuality among the human family.[2]

Not sure I could write a better treatise. A world that puts people over profit, sees all as belonging to each other, shares in monetary and cultural resources, values art and spirituality. Sounds amazing. We are not in an empire whose success is predicated on the crushing of someone else, but a world that flourishes with the good of one another. Votes for the good of others. If I get to make up the world . . . imma make it like this. Buuut, I'm a Libertarian sooooooo, take it or leave it. Wink.

PEOPLE

When you're a shark being scored on how well
you climb a tree you might as well be a piece of
kelp yelping at a blue whale, helpless.
Toothless tiger wit ruthless ire.
I almost talked me out of my own desires
You tried to tell them you were different—
You made for MAGNIFICENT.
But those with lungs don't get gills' significance

*I am becoming a still standing stanza the
    circumference of your comfort.
If you want to stay that then don't invite me to
    your conference
Imma speaker for the people defeating their
    conquistadors.
Telegraphing no moves like what these blinkers
    for?
My great-great gran, she mashed Machu Picchu.
Consider that an honor she even stoop to speak
    to you.
The least of you,
You surprised what two feet can do
One vision, execute! I don't know what we
    meeting for?
A couple Ls will teach you more
Than any war
Or liquor store
And you don't need a penny more to Mature.
This is meant to disrupt othering
Look across the table in their eyes and see yourself
    suffering. People.
Is just people
We are all we got an all we got is this and if this
    is just it then let's make it the best it
I suggest a redo because all we do is see through
War is beneath you.
Which, ain't finna sink in until we learn to
    scream out I need you*

I suggest a redo because all we do is see through
And if God finally speaks I bet
it will be through
people

AFTERTHOUGHT!

Okay, so I would do a disservice to my origin story, i.e., my daddy would kill me, if I didn't include the Black Panthers' Ten Points in this chapter. I mentioned earlier, and in many song lyrics, that my father was a Black Panther. I also think that so many incorrect narratives are being widely spread about who they were, how they operated, and what their hopes were that I feel it my duty to address that and add this to your thinking.

The Black Panthers offer another great example of imagining a better future. The demands they had, although completely reasonable, were absolutely preposterous given the state of our nation. At the end of the day, they were trying to institutionalize justice and service care for the fellow man. Of course, if you asked ten different Black Panther members what the Panthers stand for, you're going to get ten different answers. If you combine this ten-point manifesto with the idea of the aforementioned Beloved Community, you can see how listening to the people on the margins can help you better understand not only the sickness inside of our culture but a path to healing.

THE BPP TEN-POINT PROGRAM

I. WE WANT FREEDOM. WE WANT POWER TO DETERMINE THE DESTINY OF OUR BLACK AND OPPRESSED COMMUNITIES.

We believe that Black and oppressed people will not be free until we are able to determine our destinies in our own communities ourselves, by fully controlling all the institutions which exist in our communities.

2. WE WANT FULL EMPLOYMENT FOR OUR PEOPLE.

We believe that the federal government is responsible and obligated to give every person employment or a guaranteed income. We believe that if the American businessmen will not give full employment, then the technology and means of production should be taken from the businessmen and placed in the community so that the people of the community can organize and employ all of its people and give a high standard of living.

3. WE WANT AN END TO THE ROBBERY BY THE CAPITALISTS OF OUR BLACK AND OPPRESSED COMMUNITIES.
We believe that this racist government has robbed us and now we are demanding the overdue debt of forty acres and two mules. Forty acres and two mules were promised 100 years ago as restitution for slave labor and mass murder of Black people. We will accept the payment in currency which will be distributed to our many communities. The American racist has taken part in the slaughter of our fifty million Black people. Therefore, we feel this is a modest demand that we make.

4. WE WANT DECENT HOUSING, FIT FOR THE SHELTER OF HUMAN BEINGS.
We believe that if the landlords will not give decent housing to our Black and oppressed communities, then housing and the land should be made into cooperatives so that the people in our communities, with government aid, can build and make decent housing for the people.

5. WE WANT DECENT EDUCATION FOR
OUR PEOPLE THAT EXPOSES THE
TRUE NATURE OF THIS DECADENT
AMERICAN SOCIETY. WE WANT
EDUCATION THAT TEACHES US OUR
TRUE HISTORY AND OUR ROLE IN
THE PRESENT-DAY SOCIETY.
We believe in an educational system that
will give to our people a knowledge of
the self. If you do not have knowledge of
yourself and your position in the society
and in the world, then you will have little
chance to know anything else.

6. WE WANT COMPLETELY FREE HEALTH
CARE FOR ALL BLACK AND OPPRESSED
PEOPLE.
We believe that the government must
provide, free of charge, for the people,
health facilities which will not only treat
our illnesses, most of which have come
about as a result of our oppression, but
which will also develop preventive medical
programs to guarantee our future survival.
We believe that mass health education and
research programs must be developed to
give all Black and oppressed people access to
advanced scientific and medical information,

so we may provide ourselves with proper
medical attention and care.

7. WE WANT AN IMMEDIATE END TO
POLICE BRUTALITY AND MURDER
OF BLACK PEOPLE, OTHER PEOPLE
OF COLOR, ALL OPPRESSED PEOPLE
INSIDE THE UNITED STATES.
We believe that the racist and fascist
government of the United States uses its
domestic enforcement agencies to carry
out its program of oppression against Black
people, other people of color and poor
people inside the United States. We believe
it is our right, therefore, to defend ourselves
against such armed forces and that all Black
and oppressed people should be armed for
self-defense of our homes and communities
against these fascist police forces.

8. WE WANT AN IMMEDIATE END TO
ALL WARS OF AGGRESSION.
We believe that the various conflicts which
exist around the world stem directly from
the aggressive desire of the United States
ruling circle and government to force its
domination upon the oppressed people of
the world. We believe that if the United
States government or its lackeys do not cease

these aggressive wars it is the right of the
people to defend themselves by any means
necessary against their aggressors.

9. WE WANT FREEDOM FOR ALL BLACK
AND OPPRESSED PEOPLE NOW HELD
IN US FEDERAL, STATE, COUNTY,
CITY AND MILITARY PRISONS AND
JAILS. WE WANT TRIALS BY A JURY
OF PEERS FOR ALL PERSONS CHARGED
WITH SO-CALLED CRIMES UNDER
THE LAWS OF THIS COUNTRY.
We believe that the many Black and poor
oppressed people now held in United States
prisons and jails have not received fair and
impartial trials under a racist and fascist
judicial system and should be free from
incarceration. We believe in the ultimate
elimination of all wretched, inhuman penal
institutions, because the masses of men and
women imprisoned inside the United States
or by the United States military are the
victims of oppressive conditions which are
the real cause of their imprisonment. We
believe that when persons are brought to
trial they must be guaranteed, by the United
States, juries of their peers, attorneys of their
choice, and freedom from imprisonment
while awaiting trial.

10. WE WANT LAND, BREAD, HOUSING, EDUCATION, CLOTHING, JUSTICE, PEACE, AND PEOPLE'S COMMUNITY CONTROL OF MODERN TECHNOLOGY.

When, in the course of human events, it becomes necessary for one people to dissolve the political bonds which have connected them with another, and to assume, among the powers of the earth, the separate and equal station to which the laws of nature and nature's God entitle them, a decent respect to the opinions of mankind requires that they should declare the causes which impel them to the separation. We hold these truths to be self-evident, that all men are created equal; that they are endowed by their Creator with certain unalienable rights; that among these are life, liberty, and the pursuit of happiness. That to secure these rights, governments are instituted among men, deriving their just powers from the consent of the governed; that, whenever any form of government becomes destructive of these ends, it is the right of the people to alter or to abolish it, and to institute a new government, laying its foundation on such principles, and organizing its powers in such form as to them shall seem most likely to affect their safety and happiness. Prudence, indeed, will dictate that governments long established should not be changed for light and transient causes; and, accordingly, all experience hath shown that mankind are most disposed to suffer, while evils are sufferable, than to right themselves by abolishing the forms to which they are accustomed. But, when a long train of abuses and usurpation, pursuing invariably the same object, evinces a design to reduce them under absolute despotism, it is their right, it is their duty, to throw off such government, and to provide new guards for their future security.[3]

TERRAFORMING PROJECT 5

1. REGISTER TO VOTE. Then vote in all elections, and especially local elections.

2. REMOVE YOUR PRIVILEGE. Spend two days where you remove from your life at least one privilege that you take for granted. Here are some suggestions:

   − Try to get through a work/school day without your own internet access. You will have to find a way to get online;

most go to a library or other public sources.

- Remove access to personal transportation. Use public transportation. Can't just use Uber or Lyft!

- Remove access to the washer and dryer and use a laundromat. Can't just go to Mom's house either!

- Try to stack all these things together. No access to the internet, no car, and no washer and dryer.

- Function as if you are in a wheelchair. Don't actually get one because that sucks! But look out for handicap parking spots, as well as the amount of ramps and access to the places you go.

Keep a journal (or even notes on your phone) about who you see throughout the day and the emotions that arise. These exercises might help put you in someone else's shoes, which will inform how you cast votes or lobby for things that make someone else's life better, not just your own. It also might just cause you to, oh, I don't know, love your neighbor.

REMEMBER THE QUIET

What is prayer but a focused awareness
of what was always there.
So Relax. Remember. Breathe.

Anything moving makes waves
Waves are tone
The Earth moves
The Earth has a tone.
But you can't hear it
You're moving too loud.

REMEMBER
THE FIRST TIME

It was one of those gigs where I could tell I probably wasn't the first choice for the organizer. A high school summer beach camp or something. I'm hardly the party rocker LMFAO type so my music wasn't really a good fit for the event, but they paid very well and put us in a high-rise beach hotel so why would I say no? DJ Efechto and I were relaxing at the hotel before sound check. Efechto, a bona fide sneakerhead, known among many other things for his forearm tattoo of a six-shooter revolver with the word *Kindness* inscribed on the barrel (get it? Kill 'em with kindness?!), is a gentle man of few words. I refuse to tell you his Enneagram number for fear of Enneagram-related talk fatigue. He never really pontificates so when he speaks, he's prolly been thinking about what he's going to say for a long time. This day, out the clear blue, he says, "Yo, what's your earliest memory?"

Whoa, I thought. *What a question! This guy loves to cook and DJ. I'm supposed to be the thought leader and this fool drops the most profound question I've been asked in a long time!* I thought of a few things, like those car rides home I wrote about a few chapters back, the rides from Grandma's house where we would stop at the original Fatburger stand on Western. Specifically, I remembered the jukebox at the Fatburger. The jukebox's smell and sound quality. I remembered the O'Jays playing in the background of pretty much everything. I remembered Echo Park Lake, and the cigarette smell in my uncle Sonny's Eldorado. I pressed myself harder: I remembered my crib in my aunt NeNe's house on 87th and Broadway. I remembered the moment I realized that my foot was actually my foot.

I remembered observing the world around me and taking my time to process what I was seeing. How quiet and peaceful it was in my brain. Everything I saw was the first time I saw it. Every thought I had was the first time I thought about it. Peace, wonder, curiosity, no assessment or judgment, just quiet observance. No matter how wild my surroundings were, my brain was quiet. It was nice. I was about to answer Efechto when I realized, I could never have that kind of quiet again. I know too much now. I've observed too many things, I've experienced too many ups and downs, hurts and wins. There is now a grid for me to put all information through, because now I know what I'm looking at. I answered him, then mourned this loss a little.

We live in a time when information is being fired at us at breakneck speed. In a time so reminiscent of the war on drugs and civil rights, where I've found my very personhood and value being challenged. In a time where I actually have to explain that caring for Black lives is not to the detriment of anyone else's lives. Where the police lynch Black men on camera with no fear of punishment. Where the invention of alternative fact, post-truth has become mainstream, and where science takes a back seat to political expediency and to whatever the hell an "influencer" is. (All those white people in the woods, I guess.)

These days, my brain is never clear, no matter my location or surroundings. My life is the complete opposite of my earliest memories; it's always loud in my head. I was once a carefree kid in the middle of a wild environment. Now I've made a lil money, and my environment is considerably more comfortable than then, but my brain is the Wild West.

Somehow we gotta figure out how to know what we know and still know quiet.

I've dedicated this whole chapter to remembering the importance of quiet and making it a regular part of our lives. Our world has become noisy, our brains have become noisy, there is noise coming at us from every direction. But if we're building a better world, we need to quiet down the noise so we can focus on what matters. So we can listen. So we can breathe. So we can *be*.

During the 2020 presidential election, we all, as per our American traditions, sat down to watch the two candidates for president debate each other. Ask anyone if they can share one single thing they learned from that debate about either candidate's plans for bettering the nation. I'll answer that for them: NO! Instead of having a better understanding about their policies and plans, all we saw was yelling, constant interruptions, and talking over each other. It was just noise. Honestly, I think this same thing happens in our own heads. We all want a better world and probably have amazing ideas (and also probably some terrible ideas), but there's no way to know because it's so loud in your head.

Dreaming up something better requires you to quiet down everything else. How can you terraform the world if you can't even hear your own thoughts? I want to walk you through a few key things to pay attention to, to remember, in this chapter.

For myself, the quieting of the noise in my head revealed a few truths that I refer back to in my own terraforming project at the end of the chapter. I know that difficult moments won't kill me so I can remember to be like the Stoics. I know that justice is a marathon not a sprint so I can remember to be humble. I know that diversity and empathy are our greatest assets, so I can remember to love my enemies. I know the past doesn't always dictate the future. I know that people are much more complex than we want to admit, and that history is a great teacher but not a fortune-teller. At least, I think I know these things. Sometimes my mind is far from my soul. But I have learned to rehearse these truths. So here is my refrain: Relax. Remember. Breathe.

REMEMBER THE STOIC

Paul lowkey Stoic
Be content with all stages
Main or side is fine

Do not be anxious about anything, but in every situation, by prayer and petition, with thanksgiving, present your requests to God. And the peace of God, which transcends all understanding, will guard your hearts and your minds in Christ Jesus.
—PHILIPPIANS 4:6−7 (one of Paul's letters)

To all the theoBROgians, I'm aware that Paul ain't a Stoic. But let's be historical for a second. The Stoics were a crew of philosophers that were contemporaries of Paul. Like we discussed in the "Institutional Neighborliness" chapter, Paul pulls from, quotes, and makes references to the pop culture of his time all the time. I'm no Paul-stan (here's me doing the culture reference thing), but I will say I admire the way that he could swing conversations among his high philosophy audience and also his hood audience. The fact that he wrote these letters in some form of Greek, which would be equivalent to "slang," and yet still communicates the high concepts is a testament to his mastery.

Stoicism, as defined from a popular website called the Daily Stoic, "has just a few central teachings. It sets out to remind us of how unpredictable the world can be. How brief our moment of life is. How to be steadfast, and strong, and in control of yourself. And finally, that the source of our dissatisfaction lies in our impulsive dependency on our reflexive senses rather than logic. . . . Stoicism doesn't concern itself . . . with complicated theories about the world but with helping us overcome destructive emotions and act on what can be acted upon. It's built for action, not endless debate."[1]

I find it pretty fitting that Paul would appeal to some of this in this particular letter to the Philippians because one, he's pretty old now and with age comes an understanding that "F's to give" is a nonrenewable resource so use them wisely, and two, he's in jail and has a lot of time on his hands. Paul knew that becoming fully earthling takes constant becoming, a "pressing toward the mark," to use his words.[2] He knew that the people he was writing to were aware that being anxious for nothing, i.e., having no concerns, was not a destination you were going to get to and stay at forever, but rather it's the streets we drive on.

To make things more complicated, when you love others, by default that creates concern for those you love. So how can I experience both love and zero concern/anxiety at the same time? The answer, Paul says, is prayer and thanksgiving, with a call to guard your hearts.

So is the problem solved? Just tell everyone who suffers from anxiety that they just need prayer and thanksgiving and they'll never worry again? Nah, son, that ain't it. He's presenting a way, a "becoming." I know this because of the next verses, where he presents not a task to complete, but a practice: "Finally, brothers and sisters, whatever is true, whatever is noble, whatever is right, whatever is pure, whatever is lovely, whatever is admirable—if anything is excellent or praiseworthy—think about such things. Whatever you have learned or received or heard from me, or seen in me—put it into practice. And the God of peace will be with you" (Philippians 4:8).

Relax. Remember. Breathe.

———

We often don't need new info, but reminders.
It would be my honor to be your reminder.

———

MOUNT COMPARISON

When he lost his footing climbing the comparison
*   mountain*
He thought himself ill equipped to summit.
"What do them have that I don't?"
The question thunder clapped the clock hands
And gave pause.
Silly me, he thought.
He was asking the question backwards
"What do I have that them don't?"
The answer is his superpower
He has himself
Rather than using his powers to climb
He remembered
He don't even like rock climbing

REMEMBER THE HUMBLE

All beauty is an expression of the one beauty.
—JEAN KLEIN (*Transmission of the Flame*)

Here's my conundrum: How do I gain knowledge and remain open? Remain quiet? I brought this dilemma into my faith. I came from my uncle Billy Ray's "church," Citizens of Zion Missionary Baptist, where the best we were getting was an A and B selection from the choir and two hours of hoopin! Then off to Centinela Church in Inglewood where I didn't understand anything, then to San Gabriel Valley Christian Center where I first heard "personal relationship with Jesus." Then, after college I discovered reformed theology, which scratched that knowledge itch I felt like I never actually scratched in my previous faith traditions. I questioned my entire faith journey once I started drinking from that Calvin fountain. I fell into the ancient trap, the notion that the notions make the man.

Terraform your brain
Cuz you are always with you
Get your mind right, son

It's all very triggering to me now. It's human na-
ture to accumulate, but what I'm not tryin to do
is accumulate knowledge like I do objects. Read,
Read, Read, Read. Learn, Learn, Learn, Learn . . .
or what? Somewhere it all just became consumer-
ism. Immaterial materialism or as the homie Shlomo
says: it's vanity. To be honest, this is what turned me
off about the culture of Calvinism in the American
church. It wasn't the theology per se, because I still
kinda rock with some of it. It was this never-ending
expectation to be "reading something." Every time
you at the conference or in the DMs or at the cof-
fee shop, some dude in a flannel holding an IPA,
or some sort of cigar and a glass of a distilled spirit,
starts playing this game called "How deep-cut can
you get with your theologians?":

Who are you reading these days, Doc? (why
y'all call everyone Doc?)

Who are your top five church fathers?

What's your thoughts on the third line of the
Westminster confession?

It's the same thing that happens around a bunch
of '90s hip-hop heads, the race to be the most un-
derground. I just felt like I was in this one-upping
game all the time. It was like all the bros from
high school all learned tulip at the same time and
now I'm just in a locker room comparing stats. It's
exhausting.

I always felt like my answer was gonna let them down. Sometimes the answer to what I am reading is, "Nothing, I'm binging a show on some streaming service," or "I'm reading a children's book to my kids," or "I'm reading about sex positions because I'm tryin to keep my marriage happy," or "I'm reading a book on fathering daughters after they start their period," or dare I say it, "I'm reading the Koran, or an atheist text, or some transcendental meditation." The better question to ask is, "What are you learning, and who are you learning from?"

These days, I find so much joy in *not* knowing. In humbling myself. Let me be petty enough to quote myself: "I know enough to know that I don't know that much." I love, as Richard Rohr teaches, that the mystery of God doesn't mean he's unknowable, it means that the knowing is inexhaustible.

Here is how I remember to keep levels in my brain from peaking. I take it all in, no judgment, just observation. I rest in the fact that knowledge is inexhaustible, so I ain't even scratched the surface. Relax. Remember. Breathe.

REMEMBER THE ENEMY

And then,
in the stillness of your bewilderment and betrayal
the Spirit whispers in your soul, "You weren't left out,
they were never really your friends
They don't even know what friend means."
And then came the calm.

Abba Zeno said, "If a man wants God to hear his prayer quickly, then before he prays for anything else, even his own soul, when he stands and stretches out his hands toward God, he must pray with all his heart for his enemies. Through this action God will hear everything that he asks."

It's not so much that the world I'm trying to build is void of conflict. Conflict does wonders for our growth. It helps us get to the best ideas, the best self. But I'd submit that conflict can be seen not as war, but as a lovers' quarrel. We have a saying in the Black community, "Don't let no one live rent free in your brain." The only people I have ever let occupy a preposterous amount of square footage in my brain are people that I don't like. My enemies. I've spun a horrible story about them and they just kick their feet up and enjoy the Narnia I built for them in my head. This is no way to live. And almost always that story I've told myself about my enemy is untrue. Or incomplete and ungracious at best. Most likely that person is bringing up something in me that I need to deal with. I want to, I need to remember my enemy is exactly the opposite. He's one of us. He is my answer to that. Relax. Remember. Breathe.

REMEMBER THE PAIN

God don't always give answers,
but you get friends.
Really good friends.
The friend doesn't hold accountable
they hold close.

Sometimes remembering is the last thing one wants to do. The past is painful. We waded through those waters in the "Tell Better Origin Stories" chapter. Ever heard of Viktor Frankl? The Austrian neurologist, psychiatrist, and Holocaust survivor who went on to devote his whole life to studying, understanding, and promoting meaning? Wrote the masterpiece *Man's Search for Meaning*? Responsible for gems like:

"Only when the emotions work in terms of values can the individual feel pure joy" (Frankl 1986, p. 40).

And "Human freedom is not a freedom from but freedom to" (Frankl 1988, p. 16).

Does that ring a bell at all?

Anyway, big homie survived the Holocaust. That alone gives him all the street cred he needs to tell me and you anything about dealing with past pain. The type of pain you don't want to remember. In his work, he talks about three pathways to find meaning: through deeds, through the experience of values through some kind of medium (beauty through art, love through a relationship, etc.), or through suffering. They are not mutually exclusive but it's crazy how he can see that suffering became an option through which to "find meaning and experience values in life in the absence of the other two opportunities" (Frankl 1992, p. 118).[3]

I am clueless how a Holocaust survivor could learn to find meaning. His work, even though I cognitively understand, makes my soul grimace. I don't know how in the world my chattel slave forefathers stayed in the game either. But I tell you what, there's no power in blocking it out. In acting like it didn't happen. No power in tracing the stretch marks all over your abdomen and not remembering you gave birth to a human, or you were big and got small or you were small and got big. There is no power in acting like three generations of men in my family have taken to the streets of Los Angeles over the death of Black men by cops! It happened. It hurts and it still hurts. But Black people have yet to be wiped out. You are still standing! No power in seeing that faded tattoo on great-grandma's wrists and not acting like hell didn't send its best champion of the twentieth century in Adolf Hitler and homie couldn't defeat her! No power in carrying survivor's guilt.

Wrap this up: If you, or your ancestors, have experienced pain and suffering . . . I salute you, I weep with you, I feel you. Although nothing can justify what you went through, the fact that it didn't take you out makes you a monument of a human being.

REMEMBER THE RONA

Virus don't see states
We must look so strange to them.
What is a border?

In the middle of writing this book, Covid-19 broke out and upended American life as we know it. Entire countries went into quarantine on some

1918 Spanish flu steez. (Side note, did you know the Spanish flu didn't start in Spain at all?! Spain was neutral in WWI so they didn't have any pressure in their press corps to only report stories of strength, unlike countries like the USA. They were the first nation to report on the flu epidemic, but it had already circumnavigated the globe by then.) I've lived through a pandemic before: H1N1, SARS, Ebola, West Nile, Zika, but I've never been quarantined.

Remember all the "2020 is gonna be my year!" memes?! I really thought it was going to be for me, as I started 2020 headlining my first festival! IN NEW ZEALAND for crying out loud! 2020 is gonna be your year all right, your year to find the cure for wanderlust! Your year to finally learn how to homeschool! Your year to finally get to know your kids.

While I don't wanna underplay any of the seriousness of the fact that Covid-19 has taken millions of lives around the world, or say that these deaths are to teach the rest of us lessons, I still do believe this is the best living example of the point I'm making in this book. In this unique time when many of us are stuck at home, some of us working, some of us laid off, some of us with little kids running around in the back of Zoom calls, others with bigger kids trying to actually learn something in distance learning, we actually have a chance to

redo culture. Restart Earth. I still believe the truth
is yelling at us all the time. The Rona just yelled
haiku! Here is what I heard:

You live together
You really don't know your kids
Make conversation

Money is not real
1.5 trillion from feds
Where's your health care, son?

The earth will fight back
Animals need space for life
Need conservation

Pride really does kill
Floridians at the beach
You gon learn today

We are all we got
Honor the social contract
What more can I say

Prisons overfilled
Much nonviolent offenders
Need the will to change

American myths
Our exceptionalism
What's the scoreboard say?

Toilet paper gone
Watch the poor know what to do
No need to hoard, K?

We could have hired
Disabled community
Telecommute days

Liberate a state
Our health ain't more important
Than your haircut, aye?

We've lost some loved ones
We learned to value our friends
Tired of Zoom calls

Watershed event
We will never be the same
Let's make new normals

Black lives still matter
Police shoot us with no fear
Punishment won't come

Relax. Remember. Breathe.

REMEMBER THE BREATH

Just breathe even if,
The bag isn't inflating.
Oxygen still flows

I used to take so much pride in being three years ahead of where I was standing. Always thinking forward. A visionary, a prophet. Not in the sense of predicting the future, but in the sense of reading what truths are written all over us and what the implications are. I spent so much time trying to understand what may be that I missed what is. "Is" became so elusive, so uncomfortable, that I began to avoid it all together. Turns out, "is" is all we got. Past is gone, future is our imagination. Be here, Prop, now. I even wrote a poem about this in 2012 and put it on my record. It's my second-most-viewed poetry piece, called "Be Present."

When you are present, you can listen to the quiet, the quiet is actually making a sound. It's called breathing. Lie down on your back. As you are breathing, you can feel the gravity pushing down on your chest as you exhale, almost like the weight of the atmosphere is pulling your chest to the ground trying to collapse you. It's just the forces of nature. It's not evil, it's just what it is. But inhaling is a sign of you fighting back. Pulling the air into you and your chest expands pushing back at the forces that feel like they are trying to crush you. And around and around. The push, then the push back. Let that breath remind you that you got some fight in you. Be anxious for nothing, my dude; your breath is your reminder alarm, this is a practice. Peace is the streets we stroll on. What a gift breath is, it pulls you into Now. Let it be said of us: we celebrated breath, we celebrated life. Relax. Remember. Breathe.

THIS

I got plans for these here cells of mine.
And it ain't to be right here.
Bc here just don't sit right
Beautiful desert sunsets.
This ain't California breezes
This is Postmated meals for one
Lonesome doves,
Explore tab,
Almost texted crazy ex
Sex with self
The waiting kills you.
I got plans for these cells.
As proven by my bank statements.

Sir, last month you spent $400 on numbness
$230 avoiding.
$500 on next month
$600 on last year
Your streaming services totaled $69.99 on
    imagination atrophy, to forget how to daydream
    for yourself
You spent damn near $2k a month in total to
    avoid the present.
Really, n——?
What's so bad about here?
I say that as someone not currently incarcerated
Or a slave
Terminally Ill
Or possibly dead.
All of our fears, we was never happy with here.
    We dreamed of other places and spaces and
    New Year's.
And I've attempted to plant a planet's worth
    of sage.
Kush
Taken sound baths
Tibetan bowls
Chronic bowls
Richard Rohr
Contemplative paths.
Ancient prayers.
Apps and phones.

Screen time
Social media fasts.
All to get me the hell out of now.
Because here is incurable
Insufferable
My fault for even entertaining that now
Could be anything but this
Not that, just this,
Memories are electrons that fire at will
And future / imagination
We both thinking of the same Tuesday but they
    are dimensions different
Leave me in my multiverse
This is unacceptable.
My photons hold picket signs
The tyranny of physics must stop
This is what democracy looks like.
DNA grassroots organize against mourning
My chlorophyll is voting nah against death.
It the waiting, the waiting
And we were just waiting for this
Misery in mystery.
Lackluster process of discovery
Trying to find comfort in no one's ever predicted
    history.
It's just this.
Lush, ugly, lovely, this.

ONE ROCK

When she lost sight of the shore
Troubled waters seemed bottomless
She slowed down
She remembered all oceans have a floor.
It's the same floor she's standing on.
Oceans are but puddles in indentations of a rock
The rock we all standing on
I ain't no basic
I'll be fine.

REMEMBER THE QUIET

I'm really starting to enjoy my alone time.
as I'm getting older
I've started to notice I'm becoming more
*   introverted*
Tryna declutter.
Finding I don't need a lot of stimulus to get me
*   over.*
And you can turn the track down.
I like it when the level's even
in my head. Sometimes I find the volume is
*   peaking in my brain.*
Stays in the red
and it's not sustainable.

Help me to remember peace of mind.
Despite what would be happening.
And hold on to the quiet.
Remember the quiet.
Help me remember the quiet.
Remember the quiet.

TERRAFORMING
PROJECT 6

I. CREATE A NEW NORMAL WITH RITUAL. I'll be the first to admit, I need ritual. It slows me down and draws me into the moment. Maybe you are like me and wake up thinking about emails, thinking about getting things done! You've created a very productive normal. Normal is work. It's get sh*t done! I've had to remind myself that productivity is not necessarily a virtue. It's great that I ain't lazy but, bruh, your very first thought when your eyes pop open is a task?!

What I started doing is giving myself a start time. Now, when I wake up, I follow a rule that the first two hours of my day be about soul care and health. Prayer, reading, meditation, yoga, workout, a pour over and a proper breakfast. Obviously schedule doesn't always allow that, sometimes I have flights to catch or deadlines, or toddlers ready to party at 6:30 a.m. But IF my habit is a morning ritual of taking care of myself, my quiet spirit will be full so that these breaks from the norm don't destroy me. Most of us are operating in the red zone of energy and peace. That's why we explode so easy. Maybe you need to make some new normals.

2. THINK ABOUT YOUR THINKING. Because we're thinking all the time, about everything, it's hard sometimes to pause and recognize what it is we're thinking about. And our thoughts drive the whole machine. Start to notice what you're thinking about. Maybe you have a thinking pattern around a particular person, like when you see them, you've already worked out in your mind how the conversations will go. You already know they are going to get on your last nerve. Or maybe you've thought that a task you gotta tackle will suck because it always sucks. Or maybe there is something that you are convinced you aren't good at.

Now, ask yourself the tough questions: Why? Why do you think the way you

do about that person or task? What's the
pleasure in it? Is there any shame involved?
Is there something in that person that you
see that actually reminds you of you? Finally
ask yourself if there is a need to change these
patterns. Are these thoughts making your
world better or worse?

3. GET A HOBBY. There are a few rules
   here. First, the hobby can't be tied to your
   professional or personal identity or value.
   It should have nothing to do with your
   income, be something that will prolly never
   make it on social media, and that you can
   afford to suck at. Another rule is that you
   should teach yourself how to do it. If you
   end up getting good at it, it's bonus. But
   find you something that being terrible at,
   it ain't gonna take food off the table or put
   someone in danger.

   I mentioned this in the last chapter, but
   I started teaching myself how to make
   cocktails. I don't watch any videos or take
   classes, I look up recipes and try them out.
   Then I try to expand and come up with my
   own. I'm getting pretty good. And even if
   they are terrible, by the fourth attempt, I
   really don't care how they taste. The point
   isn't to become a bartender. The point is to

remember what it's like to wonder, imagine, explore, and be curious. The point is to let my mind go down paths it doesn't get to go down in my work and home life.

4. GRATITUDE LIST. I'm pretty sure you're really good at rambling off what sucks in your life and the world! Try this new normal. For the next thirty days, at some point during the day, list off the stuff you are actually thankful for. I don't care if it's the fact your left pinkie ain't broke. A broken left pinkie is awful! Be grateful. I bet by the end of those thirty days you're going to get good at spotting things to be grateful for. You're going to start noticing good things as you go through your day. It's not like they weren't there all along, it's that you fine-tuned your eyes.

Relax.
Remember.
Breathe.

THE POSSIBILITY

IMAGINE A BETTER FUTURE

In my travels through the great forests of the north,
I once asked the mother Black Bear,
"So what are your feelings on the shrinking
tropical Amazon rainforests?"
She replied,
"What's a forest?"

WE FORGOT HOW
TO DREAM

Of all the things we've covered, this is the most important. The whole book was getting us to this, the possibility. And while that sounds exciting, and hopeful (and it is!), this is also the part of terraforming where everything falls apart. Why? Because we've forgotten how to dream.

We left dreaming in kindergarten. Have you ever seen a kindergartner play? Give them an object, any object, and within minutes that object has been transfigured into the greatest plaything the world has ever seen. Cardboard boxes become spaceships! Pencils become villains in the wars between crayons and markers. Paper clips tell stories to broken Legos. In children's play world, the realm of possibility has no limits.

In an article found in the National Library of Medicine called "A Riot of Divergent Thinking," Kamran Abbasi discusses the work of educationalist Sir Ken Robinson. Robinson posed the question to adults, "How many uses of a paper clip can you think of?" Most people were able to come up with eight to ten uses. The genius-level folks could think of two hundred different uses. In the book entitled *Breakpoint and Beyond*, researchers posed this same question to fifteen hundred kindergartners. Ninety-eight percent scored above genius, which means these five-year-olds were able to name over two hundred uses of a paper clip. I have a preschooler at home and I can say based on my own experience, this absolutely tracks!

The researchers then tested those same kids five years later and then five years after that, determining that the percentage dropped exponentially each time they were tested, and by the time they were adults, the same group was only able to name eight to ten uses. I also have a teenager at home, and this tracks as well! As we age, we forget how to dream. Life experience solidifies our imagination, so that all we can picture is what *is* and not what *could be.*[1]

Here's the thing though. We often think the real world is logical, rational, maybe even boring at times. But I believe reality is far more wild and whimsical than we give it credit for. So as we step into this final stage of building the world we want to live in, I want to remind you how to dream. And it starts with physics—let me tell you about the multiverse!

It may well be that the fundamental bedrock of reality is mind dependent. It could be we are creating the reality around us. Or there is a world out there independent of us. Could be. There are certain questions, the answer to which is a smile.
—ALBERT EINSTEIN

EITHER QUESTION THE MATH OR QUESTION THE PHILOSOPHY

"MULTIVERSE!"

"Huh?"

*"Whew! Oh, did I say that out loud?!
Never mind, I'll tell you in the morning."*

This is taken from a real conversation with Alma. For a few months, Alma hosted a small gathering of women at our house every Sunday night. That meant my Sunday nights consisted of getting the kids ready for bed and running a full defensive front to keep them away from their mom. (You never feel more like sloppy seconds than when you are trying to meet the needs of your children who only want their mom to fulfill said needs.) On this particular night, I completed my duties, laid my tired body down, and began to doze off. At about 10:30, I heard Alma saying her good-byes. She shut the door and began to walk toward our bedroom. I was half asleep, and I couldn't see any of this because the door to our bedroom was shut, but I knew it was Alma based on the sound of her steps. Seriously, are you really family if you can't tell which family member is coming based on the sound of the footsteps?

Alma opened the door to the room. My back was to the door but I could see the light entering the room from the living room. I felt her get into bed, then lean over to kiss me on the cheek. Love that woman! The second her lips hit my cheek, I heard a firework, which jolted me awake. I could see the room was pitch-black, and Alma was still out in the living room in the middle of her meeting. NONE OF THAT HAPPENED! Did I dream it? Was it that weird liminal space between asleep and awake? *Superfreaky,* I said to myself and went back to sleep.

Y'all, if I'm lying, I'm flying. About thirty-five minutes later (I checked the clock) I heard Alma saying her good-byes. She then shut the door and began to walk toward our bedroom. I was half asleep, and I couldn't see any of this because the door was shut but I knew it was Alma based on the sound of the steps. I'm now freaking out! I say to myself, *This lady better not come in and kiss me on the cheek . . .*

Alma opened the door to the room. My back was to the door but I could see the light entering the room from the living room. I felt her get into bed, then lean over to kiss me on the cheek. I screamed: "MULTIVERSE!"

Now that I've used the word *multiverse* three times in just a few pages, it's time to admit that I'm absolutely a science nerd. Not enough to study it in college because that's way too much math, but enough to subscribe to astronomy magazines, listen to podcasts on quantum physics for leisure, and search YouTube for lectures on curling dimensions. Real rap life, right?

The multiverse theory is the idea that running parallel to our reality are multiple other realities where events or decisions we made in our world are different there, thus spinning into another reality. For example, there may be a universe where John F. Kennedy was not killed, or where you actually married your prom date or said yes to the first job offer and not the second. The possibilities are endless as are the number of universes.

While those are all hypothetical questions, and there have been great books, movies, and TV shows that explore this theory from a fictional point of view (check out *Man in the High Castle*), the multiverse is studied by quantum physicists. Enter my leisurely strolls through Oxford lectures. A scientist named David Wallace (not the boss on *The Office* who replaced Michael Scott for a while) gave a series of lectures at Oxford back in 2015. I'm not going to get into the weeds with the science, but basically the physicists run tests with light photons, shooting them through a machine to see if the photon goes down path A or path B. What they've found is that the photon goes down path A *and* B at the same time . . . which means the photon is in two places at once. Sounds impossible? Yeah, that's what the scientists said. So they ran it again, then they ran the math, then reran the math, then reran the tests again and again. And guess what? The photon—one whole photon, not split in two—the same photon is in two places at once.

My mind is blown! So if science is saying it's possible that there are multiple universes with multiple versions of how life could unfold for us, the question is, who hasn't daydreamed about this? A universe where you said yes instead of no to a small decision in middle school and now "other you" lives in Barbados with the most inconceivably beautiful spouse where y'all pretty much make cocktails all day and kitesurf for a living. Or a universe where you chose to go to a different college and now you're the secretary of state in the Mexican States of America (again, altered timeline) where we all are bilingual and cumbia was a required class. You chose path A instead of path B. Hopefully you love your life now, but still, how rad would it be if the spidy-verse was real?

So now we get to the point I really want to make. According to Wallace, we are faced with a choice. Either we change our math or we change our philosophy. Changing the math is basically saying, okay it's impossible to have this conclu-sion, therefore something must be wrong with the tests, or the equation is off. Happens all the time. Just rework the numbers, rerun the thing till it all works out.

Changing the philosophy, however, says, maybe our assumptions about reality are wrong! We as-sume things about reality because we've never seen anything else. But that doesn't make us right, it just means we ain't seen it before. What if the math is fine, and now we are just seeing something we never thought could be? Ludwig Wittgenstein, an old, really smart guy, is fabled to have been talking to a student, and he asks, "Why was Co-pernicus's idea that the Earth revolves around the sun so crazy for his time?"

"Well, because it doesn't look like it! When you look at the sky, it looks like the sun is moving around the Earth!" says the student.

To which Wittgenstein replies, "Hmm. What would it need to look like for it to *look* like the Earth circles the sun?"

And the answer is, it looks like how it already looks because that is what's happening. You are seeing what's happening and perceiving it a totally different way basically because we don't believe any other way is possible.[2]

I was asked once, can you imagine a world where patriarchy does not exist or racism was defeated? I tried for a second, but then I got stumped because patriarchy and racism are key ingredients when it came to the making of America. Don't kid yourself, we became a superpower superfast because we had 150-to-200-some odd years of free labor . . . slavery. Cotton was truly king. Is it not the segregation laws that gave us juke joints, that made jazz and blues? Was it not the redlining and slumlords of the Bronx that gave us hip-hop? Damn, I can't even imagine a universe without racism. But it's the very thing that my soul longs to see. Maybe my math is off? Or maybe my philosophy of what's possible is all wrong.

Change your math, or change your philosophy? Is that not the question we wake up with every morning?! Maybe you have a mental or physical routine that is not giving you the results you want to see. And so every morning your answer is try harder, figure out the formula. You wake up earlier. Eat better. Read more. Pray more. Start doing yoga. All the above. Look, maybe that is the key, you just need to figure out the math. Sometimes changing habits will change the world. But maybe you are trying to answer the question and solve problems based on an accepted and assumed reality about yourself and the world you live in. And in the next few sections of this chapter, I'd like to challenge you to consider that what is in the realm of possibility is far more beautiful than you think.

WHO YOU RUNNING FROM AND WHERE?

One-way trips?
Mind games.
One may slip?
Mind change.
One crae gift?
Is scene change.
But one may miss,
Cuz it seems strange.
Where can you go
When you the one you runnin from
Fleeing from the Spirit
Like the wind don't hear ya
Even there his hand weighed heavy on me
heaven on me,
lookin dumb while it's yellin "Who you runnin
  from?"
I insist
If my conscience would just leave me be
and just let me be me then y'all could see
I'd enlist the confidence, brilliance
Resilience of all my foremothers
I can't deny
I'm a wingspan spreading
Songbird letting
Light shine wedding
Guest list planning

Sloppy second feelin
Sexual healing
NPR donor
Tiny desk session
Second hand dressing
Love me for me!
Or don't love me at all
Boy we all go see
We find reality will always follow we
Where we roam. 360 degrees back home
One-way trips?
Mind games.
One may slip,
Mind change
One crae gift
Is scene change
But one may miss
Cuz it seems strange.
Where can you go
When you the one you runnin from

Where are we going,
where we been
We went from the catacombs to basilicas.
But once you become imperial?
Seduces even the Godliest of men.

THE POSSIBILITY:
PRODUCT WITH PRINCIPLE

Here's the thing, we live in a world of black and white, either-or, binary decisions. Or at least, we think we do. And these binaries put our imagination in handcuffs. Is it even possible to think of a government where our choices are not just conservative or liberal? Then within those binaries we gotta prescribe a value assessment, one side is good and the other is evil. What if in our new future, the one we are terraforming together, it's possible for us to operate with nonbinaries? What would that open up for us?

The reckoning with "product" and "principle" is one such binary that must be addressed. Let me be Captain Obvious. I'm an independent touring artist and author. My livelihood is dependent on me selling you books, merchandise, and songs—my product. That's capitalism. I'm also part of a people who have been absolutely crushed by capitalism. Because of this, I still feel slimy talking to people about prices. If I'm ever working at the merch table at the show, you'll see, I have a hard time looking people in the face when I tell them how much a shirt costs. I believe in my product, but making profit from it, no matter how ethical, still feels icky. Selling it, taking people's hard-earned money, still stings a little. Somewhere, I've married "product" with exploitation. I feel like I am exploiting myself, the product maker, and also the purchaser.

On the other hand, I'm also a mission-driven artist. I'm not just selling stuff because it will sell. I believe in something higher, and that my music and my art is a way to bring people into that place. In my soul, I desire to see more people take part in a higher culture. A higher culture that sees the value in the product and its purpose and willingly pays for it. That's my principle.

To that end, I believe that principle is always greater than product. But have you ever met someone so principled that they are inaccessible? I like to call them the Overwoke. The DJ who only plays the deep-cut remixes, the band that won't use digital sounds, the guy who won't play pool because the black ball gets knocked into a hole by the white ball. Principled! I feel like I gotta choose: either stand your ground with your principles, or feed your kids by selling out. Yet another binary decision. There must be a better way.

Let's bring this all together. Remember, we're all about building a world where we can dream the possibility of something looking different, and then can actually make that happen. I'm imagining a world where products are not sourced with exploitative practices, that come from a deep desire to see good in the world, and where the consumer is not manipulated into believing they need it but see the value and gladly honor the creator with their hard-earned money. One company that does this well is MiiR. They are a mission-driven drinkware company, certified B corp (businesses that meet the highest standards of verified social and environmental performance, public transparency, and legal accountability to balance profit and purpose).[3] They also focus on being carbon neutral, where the carbon emissions caused by their business have been balanced out by funding an equivalent amount of carbon savings elsewhere in the world.[4] Have you ever been to a Patagonia store? Blue Bottle Coffee? Do you have a Prop coffee cup, or a Pourigami? Those are MiiR products! The quality of these products are unmatched, *and* they are ethically sourced and sold at a price that is not exploitative. I'm telling you, it's possible to have both product and principle!

THAT'S RIDICULOUS

Product vs principle?
Economy or health
Environment or dividends
Something in me says y'all ain't gotta be enemies
But of course that's ridiculous
Of course that's ridiculous

For all of human history
Gravity undefeated
Oceans unexplored
The heavens, unattainable mystery
Soon you will launch light beams to stars
For the sole purpose of showing your genitals to a
person in a foreign land
I know, right? That's ridiculous.

Imagine the normal mode of travel will be sitting.
In chairs
In the sky
Flight will be normal and horse rides archaic
But of course that's ridiculous
A reality show president
of course that's ridiculous

It's all a simulation
That's ridiculous
Women get paid less for the same work
And people actually got murdered over the genders
    they crush on
That's ridiculous
Couldn't happen here

Another civil war
Ridiculous
Erroneous

Salacious
Sensational

At one point the trees of our planet were
   innumerable and plentiful
You moved freely through airports
Left your children to play outside
No such thing as playdates
But of course that's ridiculous

We started caring for each other
We desalinated ocean water
We be discussing how harvesting water from
   Saturn's moons could be much more cost
   efficient
Outlandish

We placed others over ourselves
We saw wars never ended so we ended the
   concept
We basically forgot borders were once a thing
Can you believe people would die over imaginary
   lines?
Our differences are our secret sauce
We had all in common
And one day we will stop being obsessed
   with stuff
But of course that's ridiculous
But of course that's ridiculous

AGAIN

Last night a Black man got lynched. Again.
By the police. Again.
This morning My folks said I should unplug from
the news cycle. Again.
Last night I tried to process. Again.
Mourn, avoid looking at his, my terror. Again.
This morning I accepted that I can't unplug when
it's mine dying. Again.
Last night they said the murder was justified
because of some past crime. Again.
This morning proved that that was a lie. Again.
Last night they said wait for facts and trust the
justice system. Again.
This morning no charges were brought on the cop.
Again.
Last night we tried peaceful tactics, T-shirts, bent
knees, silent demonstrations. Again.
This morning they dismissed us and mocked us.
Again.
Last night the language of the unheard was
spoken at the top of their lungs in the form of
burning buildings. Again.
This morning they said we were the thugs. Again.
They said follow the law. Again.
We said you first, Again.
Last night they said violence undermines your
cause. Again.

This morning we said, then why are you driving
tanks? Again!
Last week they protested government tyranny.
Last week they brought assault rifles to the
legislature.
Last week you joined the chorus of Fuck the
police.
Last week you said mandated face masks was
slavery.
Last week you protested the gov infringing your
rights.
Last week you were mad the gov was trying to
keep you alive.
This morning the government killed us. Again.
Last week you were mad the gov was trying to
keep you alive.
This week it don't matter government took our
lives.
This morning you said we were monsters. Again.
This morning you said the police ain't so bad.
Again.
This morning I'm dizzy. Again.
Nauseous
Fearful
Frustrated
Angry
Detached
Distracted

Annoyed
Pissy
Exhausted
Worried
Overwhelmed
AGAIN
Last night a Black man got lynched, by the police.
  Again.
Last night. Again.
This morning. Again.
Here we go. Again.

THE POSSIBILITY:
ALL ARE WELCOMED

I gotta share this wisdom from my homeboy DJ Mal-Ski. He says there's two ways to live: you can be Michael Jackson or Prince. If that example is too old, you can be Kendrick or Drake, Beyoncé or Badu, and if that's too urban, you can be Sufjan Stevens or Justin Bieber. Yet again another binary, but stay with me.

But back to Michael. Listen, Michael Jackson, rest his soul, is the greatest, I'm going to say it again, T H E G R E A T E S T pop entertainer of all time. He is still the gold standard. Music videos with the room full of thirty backup dancers?

Michael invented that. The moonwalk?! MJ. It's important that we come back to his personal life, but Imma set that aside for a second and focus on his professional success. Michael couldn't lose. You take all the brilliance of the team he surrounded himself with and put it on a kid who's been on a global stage since fifth grade?! Who can dance better than any living creature, with a touring and marketing budget larger than a small country's whole economy?! YOU CAN'T LOSE! A greatness so undeniable, we almost didn't notice his obvious sexual deviancy. I say that not to minimize abuse, but to accentuate how larger than life this man is.

Then there's Prince. Another musical icon. Prince just decided, *I'm gonna ride naked on unicorns. I'm gonna wear jeans with no butt. I'm gonna play twenty-seven instruments and be undeniably amazing and you will follow me. The world will follow me.* He wasn't wrong. You know why he changed his name to a symbol?! Because his label owned the name Prince so he was like . . . you can have it, I'm now "the artist formerly known as Prince" and went on to sell a bazillion albums. He changed his name to a symbol. Let that sink in!

This is the cloth Kendrick is cut from. If you notice, KDOT is not at all on social media. He don't do singles. In the season of social engagement, where scandal sells, and everyone needs new music NOW NOW NOW . . . Kendrick makes concept records. Records you have to listen through in order from start to finish! Kung Fu Kenny said, "Oh, y'all will follow me." Sufjan put out a fifty-track Christmas album?! He still sells out arenas! This route is the hopeless romantic, unquenched creative who refuses to take the popular way about anything they do.

On the planet we live on now, think about where you might land. I am hands down a Prince kinda guy. I don't flourish artistically when I feel like I need to do what everyone else is doing, only better than everyone else. I flourish when I need to think differently than the masses and make the masses come to me. And while I'm happy with the path I've chosen, sometimes I get salty at the Michaels because they seem to succeed much faster than me. I get caught in a comparison trap. And the problem with the comparison trap is that it makes you question your mojo, and keeps you from leaning into your own unique awesome. Imagine if Prince would have just followed Michael Jackson's path by having the best team and label in the world; we would have never seen the brilliance of *Purple Rain*. Some of us are Michael Jackson, some of us are Prince, but they both are legends. They changed the world.

No matter what your job is, or your skill, it's so

easy for us to fall into this comparison trap. But all that does is prevent you from sharing your Purple Rain with the world! Instead of thinking it's either go this way to be successful, or go that way to be less successful, what if we opened our thinking to the possibility that ALL are welcome? All paths, all styles, all ideas. It's like only playing two notes and then realizing you can make a much more interesting sound with a variety of notes! I'd love to see a world where we don't fall into this comparison trap. In an attempt to keep learning to love the route I've taken, one exercise I do is keep a list of artists who have never won Grammys, in order to remind me that recognition is not equal to worth. I'm about to blow your mind:

Katy Perry—zero Grammys, Brian McKnight has seventeen nominations but no wins. Nicki Minaj, Blake Shelton, Busta Rhymes. Snoop Dogg has been nominated for sixteen Grammys, zero wins. Björk has been nominated fifteen times. Dierks Bentley, Sia, Tupac. As far as legends go, QUEEN, Diana Ross, Jimi Hendrix, The Beach Boys, Morrissey, Dean Martin, Run DMC—no Grammys. I could go on.

This is zero shade to the Grammy organization or even Grammy winners. It's quite an honor, and very difficult to get one. But it reminds me that in the world we want to live in, we don't make our value assessment based on what others have done or seem to do. It's never enough, and the bar will always keep moving. Are you counting likes? Raises? Kids' successes? We all do it, but it doesn't have to be that way. And we have the power to change that. Are you a Michael?! Moonwalk into the sunset! Are you Prince? Go head and tell us how doves cry! It's all golden, it's all needed.

PITY ME

I'm not gonna always be this handsome.
This charming.
This good with feelings
This energetic.
This perfectly attuned with your needs and
*   emotions.*
And this humble.
I'm gonna fail you.

You're gonna wanna throw me out a window.
Along with everything I bought and promised.
I'm gonna fail me.
I'm gonna hide my childishness in foolish bravado
*   as if objects are eternal.*
I am going to be an ugly shell.
Abysmal pitiful picture of the man you thought
*   you married. It will be my fault.*
Oh I'll blame u.

But don't believe me.
At some point God's gonna send the hounds of
heaven to hunt me down.
In the form of dropped balls and bench warming
and torn ligaments.
Low record sales. Bad reviews and stupid blogs.
If I don't feel the sting of angelic rabies,
If I'm lucky, still wit unhurrying chase and
unperturbed pace. Deliberate speed. Majestic
instancesey,
These heavens hounds will hunt me.

I'm gonna blame you. I beg you don't believe me.
But pity me
As stars beaming with heat watch Neptune in
permafreeze
Pity me.
As pregnant clouds hover highly above the
Mojave.
Pity me.
This mortal mud suit forged of concrete and smog
Hybrid of crip walkers, Cortez and Dogtown.
When I run my calloused hand down the spine of
your confidence, know
That every awkward and painful gesture was a
failed attempt at a massage.
Pity me.
I'm crooked.
But I'm all yours.

CAPITOL I

I did the work
I had the talk
I lost the friends
I sold it off
I gave away
I let it go
I walked away
I owned my wrongs
I apologized
I ugly cried
I let others in
I got vulnerable
I forgave it
I paid what I owed.
I look at me
I like what I see
I make no excuse
I love the calm
I am clear
I like my company
And now in my head
I kinda like it here
I think I finally like it here.

I'M JUST AT PEACE WITH MYSELF. DON'T MIND ME.

I often imagine present me
Being equal parts in awe and irritated by
* future me*
I imagine future me being patient
Still enjoying the slight pauses between breaths
Consistent
Continually asking me the same question
The question I won't understand until I am him
He, we sit at the close of every day
With the eyes of an ocean of contentment
And ask me, as is his custom,
"So, what have you unlearned today?"

THE POSSIBILITY:
A BRAND-NEW CULTURE

"Okay, Prop, say it clear and make your point!" I told you earlier, sometimes I let the metaphor get in the way. So let me sum up, then cut it as clean as possible what I'm trying to say with this whole book.

Terraform. It's about building a livable world. A world suitable for human flourishing. The point of all this poetry and prose is to make us aware of what we've already been doing, the world we've been making—for good or for bad—and challenge us to be better.

And an important part of that work is building a better culture, something I've learned a lot about from William Wilberforce and the Clapham Sect. These are the folks responsible not only for ending slavery in the UK, but they are also the reason prisoners get three meals a day and outside time. They believed that virtue sits upstream from politics and culture. And who truly communicates virtue that then informs politics and culture? Artists. Art informs culture and then culture makes the human. But culture is also just humans trying to learn how to live together. Building a livable world. It's terraforming.

With each chapter of this book, I wanted to show us what we already are and what we could be. How can we build a better, more livable world? It's in the stories we tell ourselves. If the stories we tell ourselves are destructive and self-serving, then we will probably create a culture that's destructive and self-serving. After all, again, culture is us. If my stories are selfish, then we'll see the world around us as just resources rather than a gift worthy of cherishing, held as sacred.

Our lives, our home, our planet and all that it produces—the very soil under our feet—are sacred. If the world is going to be livable, we better start seeing things as sacred. Remembering that the person that is sitting next to you sprouted from that sacred soil. And he is most likely telling himself a bad story. And that one bad story is creating a culture that we all have to live in. Let's help each other tell better stories to ourselves.

Let's teach ourselves to slow down. Notice the things around us that are trying to tell us that we can be better. The truth is yelling at us all the time. Truth is that we belong to each other all standing in sacred land. Land, and all that sprouted from it, is a gift from the Divine. Like it or not, we are all we got. So maybe we should learn to treat each other with dignity and respect. As we treat each other with respect to help us to remember that trouble will come. Conflict is unavoidable. Pain will come. However, pain is a part of life, pain is a part of growth. Pain can be beautiful. Often the person standing next to you is speaking from pain. They didn't know they were a part of a terraforming project. But you do you! Relax. Remember. Breathe.

When you put all those things together you can use your prophetic imagination. Imagine what this livable world could be, then reverse engineer that mug! Tell better stories. Take care of the world around you. Take care of your neighbor. Imagine the possibility. Things do not have to be this way.

It really is in our hands, in our imagination, to build a culture that is truly livable. Not just for ourselves but for each other. Build a livable world. We make culture, culture makes us. So let's make culture awesome.

Big homie, terraform.

TERRAFORMING PROJECT 7

I. START WITH HOME. We've been talking about changing a planet, but that starts with your own space! Think of your home as its own terraforming project. What is already present in the culture of your family? What is sacred? What is life-giving? What is toxic? How can you start cherishing the things that are life-giving more while removing the things that are toxic? Who are the people in your home? Think about your relationship with your spouse and with your kids. Maybe you live with roommates; think about things that feed the idea that y'all are one, or at the least, consider how you could lead the way in making that communal space more livable.

Vision cast for your relationships and sow seeds to that. Maybe you want a home

where no one gets to say something in the
fridge is MINE, so vision cast with the
fam saying, check with others before you
eat! I have a teen daughter so I know this
is fantasy, but isn't that what we are doing
here?! Dreaming.

2. CULTIVATE A PROPHETIC IMAGINATION.
Remember way back in "Mission to Mars,"
we created a list of "it doesn't have to be this
way!" ideas? I said we'd come back to that
and now is the time!

Write a new list, this time call it a "who
says you can't?!" list. This is where we
dream of all the things that *could* be. Don't
hold back. Be ridiculous! Think of it like
a brainstorm, there are no stupid ideas.
Imagine you are five years old and that paper
clip can transform into so many things.
What could this better world look like?

Here's a few things from my list:

– An open border with Mexico

– A complete overhaul of the
  Constitution to include communities of
  color and women

– Public school having the same quality
  of education as private schools

- Kobe Bryant's birthday a national
  holiday

3. GET INVOLVED! While not everyone is
an artist or a politician, there are still plenty
of ways for you to get involved with your
community. There are some incredible
organizations out there that could use some
donations of your time and treasure. I'm not
talking about performative allyship, such
as using hashtags or changing your avi. I'm
talking about learning everything you can
about an organization's mission and vision
and following the steps to become a true
team member.

Two organizations I cosign deeply are
Preemptive Love and Food for the Hungry.
Preemptive Love's mission statement is
simple: We exist to end war. Their work
takes place in areas affected by violence.
They are at every border refugee crisis,
creating jobs, rebuilding infrastructure, and
meeting food needs. Terraforming.

I went to Ethiopia with Food for the
Hungry, a relief program that comes
alongside communities in developing
countries to help them create their own
sustainability as defined by the people on the
ground in the nations they are working in.

While many American organizations who work in other countries center themselves as the savior in the countries they serve, Food for the Hungry does a great job using their resources and access to help locally led relief projects. One example of this is the sister I met, whom I'm not naming for her own privacy. When I met her, she told me that two years ago she was gonna die from HIV. Through Food for the Hungry's child sponsorship model, a couple kids in her village got sponsored, and the village got to decide how the money would be allocated. They decided they needed help in their health and wellness, including medical care for their community.

She is now a thriving business owner who, out of her hospitality, offered to make my team and me coffee. When I say make us coffee, I'm not talking pour some grounds into a Mr. Coffee machine; this was a traditional coffee ceremony that has been perfected over five hundred years. Motherland of coffee. We all sat outside, in the space between her meager convenience store stand and her living quarters. She pulled green coffee beans out and roasted them on the spot, grinding then brewing them over hot coals. It took about forty-five minutes, but that moment was the closest I've ever felt to timeless.

So when you see these "sponsor a child" packets come by, know that it ain't some situation where one kid in the fam is ballin' out while the rest of the family is starving, or some youth group gets to paint a wall at a school. NOPE! That sponsorship meant this is a woman who was going to die, and now is alive. As a matter of fact, she's on the cover of the *Terraform* album.

Our dreams create words, our words create culture, our culture creates action, our action creates a world. A good world. A world full of possibility.

The Sky.
The Soil.
The People.
The Possibility.
Big homie, Terraform!

ACKNOWLEDGMENTS

See poems on pages 69–76.

NOTES

Tell Better Origin Stories

1. https://revenuedata.doi.gov/how-revenue-works /native-american-ownership-governance/#Indian-Tribal -Energy-Development-and-Self-Determination-Act -Amendments-of-2017

The Truth Is Yelling at You

1. https://en.wikipedia.org/wiki/Historical _revisionism

Institutional Neighborliness

1. https://www.amazon.com/Justice-Whats-Right -Thing-Do/dp/0374532508
2. https://www.asburyumcstl.org/devotions/25-traits -of-the-beloved-community
3. http://www.blacklivesmattersyllabus.com/wp -content/uploads/2016/07/BPP_Ten_Point_Program.pdf

Remember the Quiet

1. https://dailystoic.com/7-stoic-tenets-to-keep-in -mind-today; https://dailystoic.com/7-stoic-practices-to -help-you-become-your-ideal-self-in-2020
2. Phil. 3:14, NIV
3. https://www.pursuit-of-happiness.org/history-of -happiness/viktor-frankl

Imagine a Better Future

1. https://www.ncbi.nlm.nih.gov/pmc/articles /PMC3184540; https://www.youtube.com/watch?v=z

DZFcDGpL4U; https://www.amazon.com/Breakpoint
-Beyond-Mastering-Future-Today/dp/0962660523

2. https://www.amazon.com/Emergent-Multiverse
-Quantum-according-Interpretation/dp/0198707541;
https://podcasts.apple.com/us/podcast/the-emergent
-multiverse/id956859888?i=1000330762494

3. https://bcorporation.net

4. https://www.carbonfootprint.com/carbonneutrality
.html